Heritage of Power

Marie LaVeaux
to Mary Ellen Pleasant

Susheel Bibbs

featuring the praise poem *Congo Square*
by Luisah Teish

What did the mysterious vodou queen Marie LaVeaux
give to Mary Ellen Pleasant, and how did she use it
to become the Mother of Civil Rights in California?

Published by M.E.P. Publications
A division of Daya Kay Communications, Inc., Sacramento

ACKNOWLEDGMENTS

Cover Art: Original design by Susheel Bibbs,
               layout by Xochipala Maes Valdez

Cover photo: Jim Dennis (photo of Luisah Teish as Marie LaVeaux
               from *On My Journey* by Susheel Bibbs)

Book design
  and layout: by Xochipala Maes Valdez, Three Seeds Design

Editions 1 & 2: November 1998 & 2002
Revised edition: June 2011
Enhanced edition: June 2012

Library of Congress Number 98-96443
ISBN 9781892516046

Table of Illustrations

Contents

Heritage of Power
Prologue: Reasons and Thanks

Reasons

Nineteenth-century activist/entrepreneur Mary Ellen Pleasant is known in San Francisco as "The Mother of Civil Rights in California." This work, an overview of the life and accomplishments of this African-American pioneer, tells the story of her journey west, of her indigenous religious heritage, Vodou, and of what she took from that heritage with the help of New Orleans' greatest Vodou queen, "Mam'zelle" Marie LaVeaux. LaVeaux's is a colorful story in its own right—one that will have its fullest treatment in the works of others, but since one of the greatest mysteries surrounding Pleasant's life has been her alleged study with LaVeaux, this work examines her life as well in some depth.

For over 100 years, researchers have dismissed and debated a Pleasant-LaVeaux connection. So, having confirmed many aspects of it, I am pleased to illumine that connection for the first time. Along the way, I hope the motives and work of both women as well as their little-known model for social change will become clear and common misunderstandings of their lives, work, and spiritual tradition will be dispelled.

Drawing from the Source

Specifically, this book will reveal four things about LaVeaux, Pleasant, and their religious heritage:

1. that the work of both LaVeaux and Pleasant grew out of

social and political necessity

2. that both women, as priests of their indigenous faith, Vodou, worked under mandate from that faith to achieve social change.

3. that, according to research, the Vodou that LaVeaux encountered contained enough continuity and order to be called a religion rather than a cult, hence its far reaching effect in New Orleans and its ability to organize and guide the work of both women.

4. that, having studied with LaVeaux, Pleasant carried LaVeaux's model for social change, based on priestly mandates of Vodou, to San Francisco where she effected it so successfully that she became known as its "Mother of Civil Rights."

This means that one woman's work supported that of the other, although each implemented hers uniquely. It also means that the work of both women was more unified in cause and purpose than most commentators would have us believe. But who was Pleasant, and why should we care about what she accomplished?

Who Was Mary Pleasant?

Called the Mother of Civil Rights in California from work begun in the 1860's Mary Pleasant's achievements were unsurpassed until the 1960's. Pleasant was once the most talked-about woman in San Francisco. When other African Americans were rarely mentioned in the San Francisco press, she claimed dozens of full-page articles. Her dramatic deeds brought freedom to women, African American's, and others in her time. Her colorful life was part of the story of slavery, abolition, the Gold Rush, and the Civil War; she helped shape early San Francisco and covertly amassed a joint fortune in business, once assessed at $30,000,000!

However, despite her courageous deeds, by the late 1880's Pleasant and everything about her had become enshrouded in myth and obscured by legend. Pleasant grew powerful at a time when women, not to mention those of color, did not wield great power in California. And, although her charm and actions won many hearts, they also made powerful enemies who slandered her name in the tabloids throughout the late nineteenth century. Until recently, those accounts have dominated even modern reportage such that modern-day researchers have been unable to sort fact from the fiction of her life and historians have been too confounded to include her in most of their books.

Recovery of her lost memoirs and letters, along with long-hidden interviews and documents now enable us to know Mary Pleasant and her mentor Marie LaVeaux.* And, both Pleasant and LaVeaux are worth knowing because each, in her own way, was a driving force in the background and forefront of creating better lives for African Americans and others. Moreover, we care about them, not only because both had the courage to succeed while sacrificing and risking their lives for freedom, not only because one passed to the other a "Heritage of Power" (a religion and model for social change), not only because both employed superior wit against great odds to achieve their goals, but because, while achieving them, both women exhibited a love of humanity, untainted by their struggles. And, if the old Yoruba (Nigerian) proverbs apply

*also spelled LaVeau

universally when they say,

> We stand on the shoulders of those who come before us and
> Those who come before us make us who we are.

then we stand on the shoulders of Mary Pleasant and Marie LaVeaux—daring American ancestors—whose shoulders of humanity, achievement, and vision can fortify our own and help heal our divisions as a people.

One important word—In revealing that Pleasant's work was based on that of LaVeaux, I do not mean to diminish Pleasant's accomplishments. Rather, through viewing the work of both women as a response to the same religious tradition and similar societal conditions, we see that each employed her talents uniquely. Besides, the greatness of the pupil is never diminished by that of the teacher, although Mary Pleasant stood much taller "on the shoulders" of Mme. Marie LaVeaux.

Thanks

While conducting research on Pleasant's life, I received assistance from scholars, practitioners, authors, and researchers. Among them were Charles Nolan, Ph.D., (New Orleans Archdiocese), Nicole Castor, and Mary Millan (New Orleans' Bloody Mary's Tours), who shared research with me related to Vodou, LaVeaux, or her times. Thanks also to Brandi C. Kelley of Voodoo Authentica, New Orleans; historian Gerald Gandolfo and New Orleans initiates Ava K. Jones and Elmer Glover, who shared their insights on Vodou and New Orleans history; author/babalawo Fa'lokun Fatunmbi, who shared his depth of insight on Ifá and West African/Diaspora religions, and initiate Xochipala Maes Valdez, who discussed the Ifá priestess. I am grateful to them all.

I also offer some special thanks— First to author/priestess Luisah Teish, Ph.D., for her encouragement, her insights on Vodou and LaVeaux, and for the beautiful poem that she has contributed to this work. Additional thanks to two LaVeaux scholars Carolyn Long, an author/researcher from Washington, D.C., who shared many documents and insights with me, and finally, to Ina Fandrich, Ph.D. Dr. Fandrich has kindly allowed me to quote her landmark research on that mysterious Vodou queen. I, in turn, shared an early draft of this work with them in the hope that extant interviews, which I have uncovered regarding LaVeaux, might be used in their forthcoming books. Look for their works on Marie LaVeaux.

Two sets of interviews have provided keys to my discoveries about Pleasant's study with LaVeaux, and for access to them, I thank the Helen Holdredge Estate—family of the late Helen Holdredge, the dramatic biographer who preserved many valuable interviews on Pleasant's life (HH/Foley 1930, HH/Downs, 1930). These testimonies, uncovered by me in 1993 in a private home and omitted from the collection that Holdredge donated to the San Francisco Public Library circa 1977, have never before been made public. When correlated with other research, they help clarify the lives of Pleasant and LaVeaux and to dispel the common misconception that either woman's work was random.

Why Me?

Wherever I present the life of Mary Pleasant on the website devoted to her (www.mepleasant.com) in exhibits, chautauquas (enactments), or lectures, people invariably ask, Why you? Why are you doing this work?—a question I have often asked myself.

It is obvious that Pleasant, a Martin Luther King, Malcom X, and Rosa Parks of sorts rolled into one, would inspire any African-American woman. In fact, so often, when faced with a challenge, I have gained the courage to act by measuring my challenge against those of Pleasant and LaVeaux. Seeing it pale in comparison, I usually say, I can at least do that! and move forward. So, "working with" both women has helped me personally. However, most often, when people ask, Why you? they want a personal narrative.

I came to my work on Mary Pleasant after Jacqueline Hairston, an internationally respected, classical composer and arranger, asked me, as a classical singer, to consider playing Pleasant in her forthcoming opera. I responded that I would first like to discover who Pleasant was— famous last words! The opera has not yet come about, but 20 years later, infinitely richer for the experience, I am still looking into the matter.

But why could a former opera singer dare to tackle an historical research project? Well, I might not have dared had I not taken it one step at a time or had prior media experience and success. I had "worn other hats" before coming to Pleasant that prepared me for the task, including serving as a Producer and Executive Producer for WGBH-Radio (NPR station) and Television (PBS station). I recall that, as a producer at 'GBH in Boston, for example, I developed the radio series— Great American Women for the bicentennial and discovered, in the process, how much I loved historical subject matter. Later, in 1990, as an independent artist/TV producer in California, I developed a concert tour and TV documentary called An Unsung Muse on 200 years of unknown classical song of black composers—Suffice to say, I became "hooked on history," a subject I had resisted earlier in school. Both projects, had involved researching and presenting neglected subjects.

A masters-level credential in Vedic philosophy and culture gave me a love of inquiry; experience as a technical-writing manager, a documentary-film researcher/writer, and a technical-communications specialist and lecturer at the University of California, Berkeley, afforded me the research techniques for the task, so I took it on.

I guess my reason for presenting the earlier subjects was the same as for researching Pleasant's life—I dislike seeing inspiring work lost or omitted from history, especially if it relates to my people. In fact, an anger builds in me that impels me to act—one of the few things I have in common with Mary Pleasant. Then again, after painstaking inquiry, I have developed a view of the lives of both Pleasant and her mentor Marie LaVeaux—their work, motives, and tradition—that I want to share. I have uncovered the beauty of their faith, which has been misunderstood. So, to solve some mysteries that have surrounded both women and their religious heritage for many years, I wish to explain why Pleasant came to LaVeaux, to establish that she did, and to clarify their life and legacy, which have been shrouded in mystery. I hope that you will enjoy taking this journey with me to the point at which two remarkable lives and their powerful religious tradition intersected and impressed our nation.

Chapter 1: The Origin of Her Ways

The story of Marie LaVeaux, the most famous vodou queen of New Orleans, is still being unraveled by researchers, but much of Pleasant's story, distorted for so many years, can now be detailed quite easily. That mysterious time before Mary came to the mysterious Vodou queen, Marie LaVeaux, is where it all began.

The Early Years

Pleasant dictated three sets of memoirs, the last two recently uncovered. Although her first memoir was declared lost in 1993 by its most recent owner, its scribe Charlotte Dennis Downs chronicled its content in 1930 in a series of interviews with Mary Pleasant's biographer Helen Holdredge. Downs, the daughter of one of Pleasant's close associates, reported that Mary Ellen Pleasant was born a slave in Georgia. Other accounts and records show that she arrived in San Francisco in 1852 to escape persecution as a slave rescuer under the Fugitive Slave Law of 1850 (H/R: Ships Passage, vol. 3). However, by all accounts, the courage to fight for equality for herself and for her people started many years earlier.

At birth, Mary had no legitimate surname. In her first memoir, she reported being the illegitimate child of John H. Pleasants (a Virginia governor's son) and an enslaved Vodou priestess of St. Domingue, now called Haiti (HH/Downs 1930; HH24:1952). If it is true, this means that Mary had to create a name for herself. If it is also true (as Downs reported) that Mary witnessed the maiming and subsequent death of her mother at the hands of a plantation overseer, then Mary's willingness to fight slavery at all costs becomes understandable. However, the origin of her ability to love all people is not as apparent.

In the first memoir, Pleasant said that, at about the age of nine, a sympathetic planter purchased her out of slavery. No one knows if this is true because Mary tailored different memoirs at different times to counteract the gossip and criticism leveled against her in the press. Pleasant was a survivor. In the cause of equality for herself and her people, she often lived in the worlds of privilege (as a spy) and want (as an advocate) simultaneously. Living covertly often called for camouflage, and Pleasant became a master of it, both physical and verbal. In fact, in her 1887 memoir (her second) she openly declared, "Some say that words are made to reveal feelings; I say that words are made to conceal them."

Yet, although in her three memoirs she varied her story (parentage, birthplace, and the year of her birth), she never varied with regard to Nantucket. Circa 1827 on that little island off the coast of Massachusetts, Mary was to find a home and to take the shackles of slavery off of her mind to become leader, liberator, and entrepreneur. Later, in San Francisco, she would declare, "I'd rather be a corpse than a coward!" But her courage, rooted in slavery and watered in Nantucket and New Orleans, merely blossomed in San Francisco.

Legacy of Love

According to her second memoir, Mary was indentured in Nantucket (being "bounded out," she called it) for nine years to a Quaker merchant, whom she called only "Grandma Hussey." According to Mary's third memoir (Davis: 1901/02; Pandex, 1901), Grandma Hussey ran a huckster shop (a general store) that sold, as Mary put it, "everything from fishhooks to a ton of coal." Mary, by her own accounting, was fair enough in her youth to be mistaken for a white child, but she reported that her sharp mind and wit mattered more than looks in bringing "custom" (business) to the store. Said Mary of her work as a clerk in Grandma's store,

> *I could recall the accounts of a whole day and set them down,*
> *and they would always be right as I remembered them.*

Her wit and "record" memory served her well in Nantucket.

Immediately after arrival there, Mary took the name Mary Ellen Williams, naming herself after kindly Ellen, the wife of the not-so-kindly silk merchant, Louis Alexander Williams, with whom she had been placed in Cincinnati. Mary's first memoir says that the planter who liberated her from slavery, himself a Missouri slave owner, feared being criticized for educating a former slave. Thus, after only one year he removed her from New Orleans' Ursaline Convent, where he had first placed her for service and education, to the home of his friend Lewis Williams in Cincinnati. Sam P. Davis, Pleasant's final biographer, speculated that the planter must have owed Mary a great favor, perhaps having bought her because she had once saved his life. We shall never know.

We also know little about Williams, her second caretaker. He was a merchant but, according to a letter (W. Gardner 1958; Downs, 1930), he was apparently in debt. This led to speculation that he indentured

Mary with "Grandma" to work off a debt; however, according to scribe Charlotte Dennis Downs, Mary merely said that Williams indentured her to rid himself of her insolence—something she displayed purposely to protest his treatment of Ellen, his wife (Downs 1930). Either way, Mary was consigned to Nantucket for nine years, and according to author Helen Holdredge (HH:1953), she commemorated her bond with Ellen by adopting her name.

Despite being indentured, the girl who then called herself Mary Ellen Williams felt loved by Grandma and the extended Quaker family that lived with her—Phoebe Hussey, Sr., Phoebe Hussey, Jr., and (by 1840) Phoebe, Jr.'s husband, sea captain Edward W. Gardner with his two sons, Thomas and William (Davis 1901). In the light of their love Mary flourished such that, when her nine years of unpaid service ended, she chose to remain with them in Nantucket. Her guardians had become her family, and she had learned to love them.

But who were these people—these Nantucket Quakers? They were abolitionists and entrepreneurs, active in the Underground Railroad and shrewd in business. They believed in the equality of man and did something about it, even while making money (Hussey 1903). Not surprisingly, their bold spirit of abolition and enterprise also flourished in the woman later called Mary E. Pleasant.

Fighting to Be Free

Circa 1841, months after Mary's closest friend, Phoebe, Jr., and Captain Gardner were married, Phoebe helped this bright twenty-something young woman become a tailor's assistant in Boston. There Mary discovered a talent for business, a love of music and singing that would remain with her until she died, and for the first time, her charms as a woman. There she also became known as a fine seamstress and soloist—a paid church soloist. She wore her own stylish designs and attracted many suitors. "I was spritely and handsome, even if I do say it," she declared, unabashed, in her final memoir.

In short order, she doubled tailor Jackson's business by attracting suitors to his shop. This is where she eventually met her first husband, James W. Smith, an abolitionist who was fascinated by her. Reports conflict as to who first spotted or pursued whom, but by all accounts, their relationship advanced quickly. They were married circa 1842 by best calculation, despite existing reports that they married as early as 1838.

According to Mary's most compelling letter, a six-page fragment that survives in a private California collection, James, a mulatto (part Cuban mulatto, part white) was known simply as Cuban. However, in addition to being a successful merchant/contractor, he secretly spied for the Underground Railroad—the trackless series of homes and courageous volunteers who helped escaped slaves to freedom. While on the railroad, James rescued escaped slaves and reported the plans of Southern plantation owners to William Lloyd Garrison's abolitionist paper *The Liberator* .

However, although Mary depicted Smith as a daring man, she painted a picture of him as a controlling husband, dominated by his mother. She also plainly revealed her distress when, as a young bride, experiencing freedom for the first time, she experienced Smith's repression—He confiscated the clothes she had made, forbade her to alert her Quaker people of their wedding, and forced himself upon her on their wedding night. Life with Smith meant a good station and an exciting life, but Smith's treatment after their marriage led Mary to mourn, "All I felt was that I had somehow lost my liberty all over again." And, although she claimed in her final memoir that she grew to love him, she also jokingly planted a doubt by adding, "but with James I lost my say, and I always had to have my say!"

Mary supported James' efforts on the Underground Railroad by entertaining abolitionists in their Boston and Virginia homes and by traveling with him at times to Philadelphia and Ohio, the state James first called home after his father, an ex-governor, removed his family from Virginia to freedom in that state. From James, Mary "learned the ropes" of abolition, and though she resented his control, she admired him and remained grateful to him for his example.

James' area of operation without Mary, however, ranged from Nova Scotia to his property in Charlestown, Virginia (now West Virginia) near Harper's Ferry. There, according to Mary's six-page letter fragment (Letter dictated to Mrs. S., undated), his white father had left him a plantation. Few property records in that area are available before 1861, but according to Mary's letter, James' plantation was serviced, not by slaves, but by men whom he had bought and freed. Thus, even though he did not seem to accept Mary's right to freedom, James cared deeply about liberty, such that he would pay as much as $1,000 to set a slave free (ibid, undated).

After several years of intense travel and work, James became ill. However, because he was abusive to her and because his death came suddenly, some have said that Mary "had a hand in it." Downs even states that Mary once admitted it, and a second-hand report says that her second husband suspected it. However, nothing was ever proved. Mary merely says that in 1844 Smith left her a wealthy widow—free and secure for the first time in her life (ibid), that she sold their Virginia plantation, and that, with the help of Captain Gardner, she cashed in Smith's bonds to the tune of $45,000 in gold; this she vowed to use "in the cause of the colored race" (Davis: 1901).

Legend has it that, in the years that followed, Mary became notorious as a slave rescuer, working out of Railroad headquarters in New Bedford, where she and a second husband eventually relocated (New Bedford Census, 1850). During those years, she stole onto plantations disguised either as a man or a Negro jockey to alert slaves of impending escapes. There is no proof of this, but Mary was no stranger to covert activity. Slaves covertly maintained their religious and cultural heritage and used it to escape and to survive, so Mary surely understood the importance of covert action and secrecy. Yet she admitted using it only in her final days (MEP/Davis: 3/1902). Covert action demanded courage, and Mary seems to have acquired hers by James' example and by fighting the demons and pain of her past. Hence her motto,

I'd rather be a corpse than a coward (Michelson: SF Call 1901).

Moving On
Fugitive

In 1850, California petitioned to enter the Union as an anti-slavery state. According to historians, one reason was to discourage slavers entering the state from bringing in slaves, who might work the gold mines to unfair advantage (Templeton, 1993). Since California's entry threatened to tip the even tally of pro-slavery and anti-slavery states in favor of the anti-slavery faction, Senator Henry Clay proposed the Compromise of 1850 to appease the pro-slavery states. This included the Fugitive Slave Law. Essentially the Law (or Act as it is sometimes called) enforced older fugitive slave laws by allowing bounties for fugitive slaves and rescuers, setting up adhoc courts, and for Mary, bringing increased pressure to bear on slave rescue activities. Consequently, with slavers hot on her trail, she ultimately fled west.

This flight, however, is sketchy. In 1849, just before the Law was enacted, Mary escaped slavers by hiding out in Nantucket with the Gardners. After the Law, according to Mary and a letter by Captain Gardner's son, Thomas, Gardner helped Mary escape to San Francisco (Delaca/Gardner1905). However, sometime before she journeyed west in 1851, Mary had remarried and lived in New Orleans. Thus, the western flight actually seems to have occurred in stages.

Second Husband

In her last memoir, Mary reports that Smith's mother suggested her marriage to Smith's former foreman and close friend, John James (JJ) Pleasance. Downs, however, reports that the first memoir spoke of a strong attraction between Mary and JJ. From the beginning, however, their relationship was probably a mixed bag. According to Downs, JJ's sensuality fascinated Mary, but according to Mary, JJ dressed loudly and "wasn't half the man my first husband was" (Davis: Pt.2 1902).

What little we know of JJ Pleasance comes from Mary's memoirs and brief testimony by his associates. We know that he was handsome and had hazel eyes. He once reported first seeing Mary as she attempted to conduct a Vodou ceremony, perhaps on her plantation. He considered himself a "free man of color," related also to Creoles in Haiti and New Orleans.

The term Creole, originally used for persons of European descent, born in Louisiana, currently refers to them, their Haitian relatives, their offspring, and anything/one who originated in New Orleans before the Americans purchased Louisiana in1803. John James was not, however, related to Mary's father John H. Pleasants, as some have claimed. Rather, he thought himself descended from Emperor Henry Christophe of Saint Domingue (now Haiti) (HH24/25: Camba; WWJr., Downs; Delaca/ undated).

JJ's story was intricate, but not unusual. According to New Orleans historian Gerald Gandolfo, after 1820, when the Americans had taken firm control from the Creoles in New Orleans, many Creoles relocated to Haiti to escape the political and social pressures of the new American regime. Once in Haiti the Creoles patronized its Emperor (Christophe) and were, thereby, allowed to move freely there (Gandolfo, 1996). Simply put, JJ's father (Emperor Christophe's illegitimate son by a white mistress) was said to have been named Pleasance [Plaisance] as a tribute to such a Creole patron—if not as a tribute to Plaisance, Port Cap Haitian—a place that the Emperor loved. JJ was, therefore, a Christophe by birth. Remarkably, James "Pleasance" was eventually sold into slavery to Mary Pleasant's paternal grand father —an ex-Virginia governor named James Pleasants, who owned a plantation called Contention. This ex-governor later freed James Pleasance and his son John James (JJ)—the man who would become Mary Pleasant's second husband. So JJ was rightfully a "Christophe."

Still, Mary wanted the Pleasance surname because it could be Anglicized to "Pleasants," her father's name. And she once said that she married JJ to get her name (HH/Downs 1930). However, as a "Christophe," JJ offered her other gifts. He had distant Creole cousins (friends and family, white and "colored") in New Orleans, among them Louis Christophe Duminy du Glapion, the white Creole husband of Mam'zelle Marie LaVeaux.

Time to Stay

Some time after their marriage and arrival in New Orleans from Nantucket, JJ became a ship's cook and left Mary so that he could scout a safer, more prosperous life for them in California gold-rush country. Mary stayed behind to "own up" her religious heritage and to arm herself with the "secrets" of Mam'zelle Marie LaVeaux. Mary later told the story to several close associates, but she wrote about it only once (HH24, 25: Downs, Francis; Downs, 1930).

Charlotte Downs' report of that "writing," as the scribe for an unfinished, dictated memoir, says that Mary's mother, as a Haitian Vodou queen, had held a shaman-like position, which mandated healing skills, a knowledge of ritual, and social responsibility for her community (Desmangles, 1992). Mary was to have inherited this priestancy; however, Mary's mother had been killed for practicing her faith on the plantation (troublemaking) and so could not complete her daughter's training. Thus, apart from preparing her for abolition activities in the West, study through "the Christophe connection" with a famous, social-activist Vodou queen should have meant a lot to Mary personally. Later when social ridicule made the association seem burdensome, Mary the survivor, simply edited it out of her story, though not out of her life and work.

Photo identified in the 1930's as Pleasant by seven of her close associates and labeled "Mrs. Pleasance" in SF Detective I.W. Lees' collection. Some say the photo is actually Queen Emma of the Sandwich Islands

Chapter 2: Lost Legacies

Solving the Mystery

Mary Pleasant's study in New Orleans has remained shrouded in mystery. In fact, that part of her life journey was confirmed only in 1930 when dramatic biographer Helen Holdredge gathered first-person and eyewitness testimony about it. However, she never published her sources, so historians have remained uncertain about it. As part of a depression project Holdredge interviewed two women. One was Pleasant's scribe, Charlotte Downs, who grew up around Pleasant's household in the late 1870's and early 80's; the other was Liga Foley, a woman of 95+ years who thought herself to be the granddaughter of Mam'zelle Marie LaVeaux (HH/Foley 1930; Teish 1985:170). Although they did not know one another, the Downs and Foley interviews corroborate one another, helping to confirm the final, pivotal step in Pleasant's early life.

Liga's Tale

Taking a Look

The second woman interviewed by Holdredge, Liga Foley, should speak first because hers is an eyewitness account. That is, whereas Downs simply recalled what Pleasant had told her, Liga recalled the events first hand. For example, Charlotte said,

> *Hardly known was that "mammy"* learned Vodou from Marie LaVeaux in New Orleans. Her husband—that is "mammy's" husband—was in some way connected with the man that*

---

* Pleasant hated this derogatory nickname, popularized in the press by her enemies.

> *Marie was living with at that time, and who was the father of*
> *her children.*

Liga corroborated, giving eyewitness detail,

> *I know what Mrs. Pleasants look like. I saw her... ('course, she*
> *was named Pleasance then, her man being related to Marie's*
> *man, Christophe Glapion, and the both of them attached to*
> *Emperor Christophe in some way). Marie was teaching Madame*
> *Pleasance Vodou...* (HH/Foley1930)

As Marie's ward, raised in Marie's home, Liga had seen Madame Pleasance in New Orleans before she herself had run away from Marie out of fear of having to succeed her as a Vodou queen. Liga arrived in San Francisco in 1851, a year before Pleasant. Once there, she worked in the exclusive Oriental Hotel in service as a tutor of French for the children of Southerners who planned to leave the States for France in the event of a civil war. From then until her interviews with author Holdredge in 1930, Liga had disguised herself as the French Indian, Anaria, speaking little English and shunning anyone who might have known Marie LaVeaux; for Liga was a "dead ringer" for her grandmother and feared being discovered.

Liga did not escape the notice of Pleasant, who at one time had to work with her at the home of Senator Latham in San Francisco; however Pleasant seems mercifully to have allowed the notice to pass after demanding a brief interview, which was harrowing for Liga. Liga also avoided Southerners, members of the Vodou faith, Pleasant, and Pleasant's associates in general. Thus when she told her tale to Holdredge, having lived in that disguise for over 75 years, the confession became a catharsis (ibid 1930).

Liga had not always known her exact relationship to Marie, but she thought herself to be her granddaughter because that's what Marie's youngest daughter, Philomene, had told her. Liga told the story this way in English that she said she had learned long ago from Marie's son, Jean, who had learned his English in the New Orleans marketplace,

Seems like I always had a suspicion I was Marie's grand daughter. Marie Philomene [Marie Philomene Glapion Legendre], Marie's youngest daughter, was cloven-footed [difficult] most time. One day when she was mad at me 'bout something, she put a blight [hex] on me, and my spirit was crushed for a long time afterward. She was never going to correct the error of her ways, and I knew a devil when I sees one. She was fixin' to bust when she spewed this out, and she was paying me off for daring to fight her. She said I was actually the daughter of Marie's first child, Delphine, and that's why I was called Dellie... Marie Philomene said she overheard Marie talking to old Chloe, and that is how she knew.

I couldn't hold my feet when Marie Philomene spilled what she knew. Chloe had dumped me onto Marie 'cause my mother Delphine said I showed "darkey blood." Her husband, my father, was a wealthy white planter. When Marie Philomene told Marie she knew all about me, Marie transferred the ownership of a house on Toulese [sic Toulouse]—the river side—to keep her mum.

Marie passed off Delphine by moving her there so she'd get no blight [color stigma] to get hit with. When Foley [Liga's white father] began to spark her [pressure], Chloe [Delphine's old guardian] let on [told Foley that] Spaniards, who built the place, must have been her ancestors... [Later] Marie Philomene was the onliest one to know what was what, 'cause Chloe was dead....

Next Liga recounted having seen Pleasant at Marie's,

I know what Ms. Plaissance [sic Pleasance] looked like. She came visiting my grandmother one day. I met her again later in San Francisco. [But in New Orleans] she didn't see me; I know this, cause I was merely peeking at her...

According to Liga, therefore, Mary Pleasant met with Mam'zelle Marie LaVeaux sometime before her own departure for the West in the summer of 1850. Thus, Liga's testimony helps us to approximate, for the first time, Pleasant's study with LaVeaux and, along with other testimony, Pleasant's departure for the West—that is, corroborated testimony places Pleasant in Nantucket in 1849, so we know that she arrived in New Orleans after that, and according to ship's records and her own memoir, she left there in time to arrive in San Francisco in April of 1852 after a few month's delay in Chile (HGR1852; Davis 1902). Further, Pleasant says that her husband JJ preceded her to San Francisco on the Flying Cloud, which sailed in August of that year (Teish 1997:136; email 1998; Davis1902). Therefore, Pleasant would have worked with LaVeaux before the summer of 1850 and left New Orleans by late November of that year. Since no records exist to verify Liga's tale or Pleasant's travels, this type of intricate correlation becomes important.

Checking it out

Fortunately many things that Liga asserts correlate with testimony or add enough credible detail to legend that her tale itself becomes believable. Below are a few more examples of the importance of Liga's story and a few more ways in which it seems to "check out":

For years a legend has existed that LaVeaux retired more than once before her final bow in 1869. Legend also says that the first time she retired (to create the impression of being immortal), she replaced herself with one of her daughters (New Orleans Commerce 7/5/1869; Teish 1985:170). Less likely (because she had already passed her crown to her successor, Malvina LaTour) are the claims that say that Marie returned to her reign after '69 and retired again in the 1870's. However, from Liga's tale, we now know that there is probably truth to the first story and that Liga was once to have been LaVeaux's replacement.

There is also a companion story that one of LaVeaux's daughters [sic] ran away with a white man and/or was eaten by an alligator (Fandrich 1994: note 41:308). In her testimony, Liga mentioned her surprise, when, during her harrowing interview with Pleasant in San Francisco, Pleasant recounted to her Marie LaVeaux's version of a similar tale. Liga clearly claimed to have been that girl when she told her interviewer,

Back in New Orleans they don't know what has become of me. I was supposed to be eaten up by an alligator...

Of course, by running away, Liga escaped being LaVeaux's stand in—a position (often called Marie II) that I believe was first filled by Marie Eloise Euchariste, Marie's daughter. Euchariste died suddenly in June of 1862 (Long: notarized archival documents), and I believe that this forced Marie out of the retirement she had taken shortly after 1860, when it is reported that she became chronically ill (Weekly Picayune 1881); hence the legend that Marie's final retirement, circa 1869, was her second. Whether my theory is correct, it is clear that Liga's tale clarifies popular legend credibly.

Another mystery for researchers, which Liga illumines, has been the disappearance of Jacques Paris, Marie's first husband. Only legend exists to explain why Paris left Marie suddenly, and no on knows what became of him? Yet Liga explained his disappearance matter of factly—

[Unknown is that] *Marie LaVeaux had had another daughter that wasn't accounted for. Her name was Delphine [Liga's mother]. Marie's mother, Marguerite [D'Arcantel], forced a carpenter to marry her because she couldn't account for her being pregnant. His name was Paris, and he came on the scene after Marie was already pregnant. Once Marguerite [who] was dying, was dead, Paris left Marie, although Marie's white father [sic], LaVeaux, had furnished them with a nice house* [207 Amour, now Rampart St.; Judgement #4597 11/28/1881 Civil Dist. Ct.].

Certainly, if forced to marry Marie by Marguerite (Marie's mother), Paris might well have left as soon as she died. Most importantly, whereas other versions of Paris's departure either implicate Marie's Vodou without proof (Tallant, ed. 1992) or simply call his departure a mystery

(Weekly Picayune, 6/18/1881), Liga's version, whether surmised or repeated hearsay, renders his departure reasonable for the first time.

Liga is the only person ever to have asserted this version of Paris's departure, but one unique detail of her account lends it credibility: Paris's disappearance has been mentioned in accounts since the early 1880's, but Marie's father's wedding gift has not. Robert Tallant in his dramatic biography of LaVeaux (Tallant, 1946, ed. 1992) was perhaps the first to mention it in print, and Ina Fandrich, Ph.D., to my knowledge, was the first to document it (Fandrich dissertation 1994). Liga mentions it almost in passing. How did she know?

Liga's amazing tale continued over the course of seventeen interviews with Helen Holdredge. In them she covered, not only her first sighting of Pleasance, but details of Marie's most secret ceremonies and motives. Two more things speak strongly in favor of Liga's tale, 1) She seems to be a reticent interview subject and 2) She was not an advocate for Marie LaVeaux. She loved her "grandmaman," but found some aspects of Marie's and her ceremonies frightening.

A small detail that strengthens her credibility is Liga's description of Marie's home on St. Ann St. Said Liga,

Ya know, her house was on a deep lot with the front yard most
shallow behind a bottom gate with a peep-hole in it...

Writer George Washington Cable, who is said to have visited LaVeaux there when the queen was in advanced age, described the house similarly—complete with shallow yard and fence,

> *Her dwelling was in a quadroon quarter of New Orleans, but a step or two from Congo Square, a small adobe cabin just off the sidewalk, scarcely higher than its close board fence* ("Creole Slave Songs," Century Magazine: 4/1886).

Of course, only Liga, who was fond of spying at visitors like Mary Pleasant through that fence, recalled the peep hole in that fence. Interestingly enough, a sketch of this cabin depicts the sort of detail that Liga might have been describing when she said,

> *-and she [Marie] added a second story, 'most like an attic, and put she kitchen by-itself, like on the plantations. She also put ship-lap [a sort of layered covering] on the outside. This [remodeling] was so she could use the parlor. Her close-tie [live-in] helper was Rose. She was provided for most kindly in a lean-to off the kitchen.*

This only known illustration of that LaVeaux cottage (shown below in this book) depicts Liga's detail—detail that other narratives fail to notice. How did she know?

In fact, one researcher whom I consulted reported (as did the artist, Cable, and interviewees in the Louisana Federal Writer's Project) that LaVeaux's home was a one-story cottage (Long email 1998; F.W.P, folio 25). However, examining the famous illustration closely, one can see a fence and the little door or window on the house that possibly marks the attic-like space that Liga described. On the side is sketched what looks like the "lean-to" kitchen that Liga described (Historic New Orleans

Collection; Bodin, 1995:23).

THE OLD LAVEAU HOUSE.

(Courtesy of The Historic New Orleans Collection)

1880's sketch of LaVeaux's St. Ann St. Cottage on which the
second-story window and lean-to described by Liga Foley can be seen

Advancing the Saga

Of course, verifying her knowledge of Marie's little cottage on St.
Anne was not the point of Liga's tale. Because Holdredge had asked her
to, she wanted to advance Pleasant's story, and so must we. Said Liga in
the quote merely excerpted earlier,

*Marie Philomene and myself had quarters in the second story... Ok,
what I'm gettin' at was the time I first spotted Madame Pleasant. -'course,*

she was named Pleasance then, her man being related to Marie's man, Christophe Glapion, and the both of them attached to Emperor Christophe [of Haiti] in some way. Marie was teaching Madame Pleasance Voodoo so she could use it in some way. Philomene and I couldn't see much—just feet in the candlelight and the snake being lifted from his box. That's when I gave up looking because I hated snakes!

Seems like I had a resemblance to LaVeaux. I had a naggin' suspicion I would be required to hold a snake over my head too if I followed in her [Marie's] footsteps, and I decided, although I didn't know where I'd be goin, I'd get out of there.... [When] the pat time [was] over, I fled out to the road, resolving I would never help Marie out by pretending to be her, to give her the reputation of being immortal.

Chapter 3: Mam'zelle's Story

Looking for LaVeaux

So Liga fled rather than act as successor to Marie LaVeaux, whereas Mary Pleasance longed to complete her training as a priestess under the great Vodou queen. But, who was this person, both feared by Liga and revered by Pleasant? Who was Marie LaVeaux? A man named Tom Bragg, who saw her, had this to say,

> *She come walkin' into Congo Sq. wit' her head up in the air like a queen. Her skirts swished when she walked, and everybody step back to let her pass. All the people—white and colored—start sayin' that's the most powerful woman there is* (FWP: folio 25).

As with Mary Pleasant, opinions vary on almost everything about Marie LaVeaux, once called "the most powerful woman there is." In fact common New Orleans lore has it that so many LaVeaux imitators arose in the years after Marie retired that confusion about her identity and accomplishments still abounds (Millan 1998). However, according to baptismal and census records, the real Marie LaVeaux Paris de Glapion, sometimes called the widow Paris, was born in New Orleans c.a.1794.

Of course, as with Pleasant, dates vary. One record and an obituary, both attributed to LaVeaux's daughter Philomene as source, have caused the most controversy because they would have us believe that Marie died at the age of 98 in 1881 (Weekly Picayune: 6/18/8; death certificate). That would mean that she was born in 1783. However, the same news account also says that she was 25 in 1819. This would mean that she was born in 1794! That year is supported by accounts given by Marie herself in several vital records; that dates seems to be correct because the man thought to be her father (born in 1875) would only have been nine years old at the time of her birth were she to have been born in 1783 (Long email 1997)!

Artist Charles Gandolfo's rendering of a young Marie LaVeaux,
Courtesy, New Orleans Voodoo Museum

Clearly, LaVeaux's early life is shrouded in mystery and myth, but some things seem clear: Her mother was most certainly Marguerite D'arcantel, also called Marguerite Henri. Marguerite, possibly an herbalist, died before 1830 (Pomet sucession; Fandrich email 4/8/98). According to Marie's marriage certificate, her father was Charles (Carlos) LaVeaux, a well-to-do "colored" Creole (free man of color). LaVeaux scholar, Ina Fandrich, believes that Charles LaVeaux was the common-law son of well-known New Orleanean, Charles LaVeaux-Trudeau, through a liaison with a woman of color. The relationship with LaVeaux-Trudeau has yet to be proved definitively, but according to Dr. Fandrich, family interactions support it (Fandrich email 3.30/98; dissertation 1994). We could say therefore that Marie's mother, father, and paternal grandfather are fairly well confirmed. The rest remains unproven.

Her father's mother is listed as "Marie" LaVeaux on his death record (Long email 1998; Millan 1998), and Dr. Fandrich has located a letter from a New Orleans botanist that identifies a root woman (herbal healer) of the same name. If these women prove to be one and the same, then the nursing skills that Marie employed so well during the plagues in New Orleans could have been her grandmother's legacy to her.

This paternal grandmother might be accounted for in New Orleans property records and death records because one record places LaVeaux's alleged grandfather, Charles LaVeaux-Trudeau in the same compound with a woman identified as "Marguerite" LaVeaux-Trudeau (Vieux Carre Survey, Lot 18472). She is listed ambiguously in a baptismal record as a woman from Guinea (if spelled correctly, suggesting an African woman, perhaps enslaved); however, she is also listed both as a free woman of color and free negress (nigresse libre)—both designations for one of mixed race, usually born free (SLC F3,122; MacDonald/Carter 1979:125). If African, she might once have been Charles' family's slave (Fandrich email 1998). Yet, the fact that she is recorded as having purchased expensive Trudeau land from Charles' brother within the family compound shortly after LaVeaux-Trudeau's parent's death, casts doubt or suggests a defacto sale of the property to her. Since LaVeaux-Trudeau is thought to have fathered Charles LaVeaux with a free woman of color (fwc), and the disparate recording of names was commonplace in New Orleans, this "Marguerite" might have been wrongly listed as "Marie" LaVeaux on Charles' death record. Such confusion regarding names and spellings was all too common in New Orleans partially due to its complex system of common-law relationships. This system bears brief explanation.

Le Placage

In the South, many Creole men were subject to arranged marriages to preserve family property or wealth. These were not always fulfilling relationships, so the society (to some extent) condoned common-law marriages and liaisons, usually with women of mulatto or African origin. Young Southern men of breeding, such as Pleasant's father, John H. Pleasants of Virginia, were sent by their fathers merely to "sow wild oats" with such girls (HH/Downs 1930), and in Haiti, French men fathered these children at random (Desmangles 1992:21-24). However, in New Orleans special arrangements were made between Creole men and these girls, which, even if not legal marriages were respected socially as such (MacDonald/Carter 1990:172-74).

Even the Ursaline Convent (Teish interview 1998) groomed girls for this status, and they were often introduced formally at special dances called "quadroon balls." After a man had selected a common-law wife, the relationship was usually formalized by a contract, forged through a matchmaker. This contracting was called Le Placage (the placing). Laws prohibited interracial marriages in New Orleans until about 1870, although, during some periods, the law was disregarded, and at times, priests performed unofficial "mixed" marriages (Long email 1998). However, the matchmaking contract was the norm in such matters.

The 50 to 60 rules called the Code Noir (Black Codes), which came to Louisiana in 1724 were followed by Spanish counterparts in 1795. These codes allowed the mixed offspring of these arrangements to live freely (Desmangles 1992:22). Under these laws, Creole men could formally claim their children and will property to them. However, according to New Orleans historian Gerald Gandolfo, as time went on, these Creole men often claimed to be mulatto to assure their children's rights. Whether live-in or absentee fathers, they also educated their offspring in Paris and gave them good jobs and property (Blassingame 1973:17,18; N.O. Census, 1850; Gandolfo interview 1996. MacDonald et al 1991:27, 122).

One wonders if Mary Pleasant ever felt that her own father, John H. Pleasants, would have made such an arrangement with her mother if Virginia's aristocratic Pleasants clan had condoned it. However, they did not. Their boy, heir to a political career and a vast Goochland, VA, plantation called Contention, fresh from law school, and newly widowed, was not to be aligned formally or informally with any Santo Domingo (Haitian) slave girl (Pleasant's mother), especially one who openly influenced him and practiced Vodou. So, Pleasant's mother (also named Mary) was banished to a seedy plantation in Georgia to have her child (HH Estate: Downs 1930). Still, Mary might have imagined that John H. Pleasants loved her mother, for we know through her scribe, Charlotte Downs, that she definitely felt she deserved the "Pleasants" name.

Marie's father, Charles LaVeaux, was certainly a free man of color and could have been the result of Le Placage. Charles, half Creole, was perhaps very fair because Liga, in her 1930 interviews, says of Marie's fine spoken French, "Her white [sic] papa sent her to France to be educated." Liga was mistaken here. Marie claimed to be illiterate, although her spoken French, given her class, probably was "perfect"—sounded very polished—as Liga said (MacDonald et al 1979:125). Moreover, Charles, her father, was not white, as was her alleged grandfather. Yet, Marie's daughter, Philomene, as the source of Marie's 1881 obituary (which Liga should not have seen) seems to have made the same assertion about Marie's father. The mistake was possible because Charles LaVeaux died in 1835 when both girls were babies. Charles LaVeaux did not live with the family, and many of his group were indistinguishable in appearance from whites (MacDonald et al: Rankin 1979:118) One might, therefore, assume that both Liga and Philomene were recounting impressions of his appearance or merely community perception. Anyway, the things said by both ladies about Charles LaVeaux are typical of the Placage arrangement that might have produced him. Le Placage certainly forged the unique community in New Orleans called the Free People of Color (fpc) to which he, and thus Marie, belonged.

F. P. C.'s

The group sometimes called the Creoles (Kreyols) of color or Free People of Color (fpc's) comprises largely the sons, daughters, and descendants of Creoles with Placage arrangements. This facet of society to which Marie belonged was complex and unique. The Black Codes (Codes Noir), instigated originally by the New-World clergy, were promulgated in New Orleans to protect slaves and mulatto's in French colonies and, among other things, made the mulatto offspring of Creoles a valid "third" class in French society (Desmangles 1992:23; MacDonald et al 1979:14). In fact, of them the Louisiana envoy of President Lincoln would one day declare to the American establishment,

The question of granting them political rights has nothing to do with the propriety or justice of conferring these rights at once upon the whole body of the emancipated slave. There is no parallel between them.

Most often educated, these "Colored Creoles" could usually speak perfect French (MacDonald et al 1979:25) and also a language of their group called Creole (Kreyol), a French patois (French, Spanish, African blend). Members largely of Saint Louis Cathedral in New Orleans' Jackson Sq., they were especially active in the social projects and missions of the City and the Catholic church (Gandolfo interview 1996).

These sons and daughters of Creole planters and landowners, usually born in Louisiana or Haiti, formed a privileged, merchant middle-class that stood between two worlds—the free white and the enslaved. Many were very European in manner and even owned slaves (MacDonald et al, 1979:122). Much has been made of their difference as a class from the enslaved, yet by 1805 some fpc's were the leaders of Vodou in New Orleans and later they would unite with the slave population on questions of rights (McDonald/Davis 1979:118-127). The question is, Why?

By 1785, the time of Charles LaVeaux's childhood and the Spanish rule over French "planterdom" in Louisiana, all fpc's were supposed to be Catholic. However, many of them (Haitian immigrants fresh from the Haitian revolution in which Vodou played a major part) had not practiced Catholicism since Catholic priests fled the Island during the first Vodou-based uprisings there circa 1791. Using Vodou, the Haitian rebels ultimately repelled Napoleon's army, freeing Haiti (Desmangles 1992:34-37), and Haitian fpc's, filled with the French Revolutionary spirit of "liberty, fraternity, and equality," were a part of this fight to protect themselves from the constant erosion of their rights, which had been taking place in Haiti since the 1760's (ibid 1991:28-29; L'Union 9/27/1862). Some were initiates (Asbury 1938:255).

Their country in turmoil after the revolution, they sought prosperity in Louisiana, the plantation site chosen to replace Haiti. Once there, especially in New Orleans, they prospered and blended with local fpc's (Marie's group). Although the fpc's would seem to have been too Europeanized, too busy as a prosperous merchant and planting class, and too comfortable overall to have cared much about social causes, the records show that they did care. They cared because, within a short time after the American take over of Louisiana, they again had to fight the continuous erosion of their rights (Desmangles 1992:24; Asbury:1938:255; McDonald/Davis 1979:125-129). Those who remained solely Catholic founded Catholic charities and organizations. However, others, just as they had in Haiti, used Vodou as a tool of the fight.

One fighter in New Orleans, by the 1830's, was the free woman of color, an initiate, named Marie LaVeaux, who seems to have been empowered by her faith. To understand what LaVeaux and other fpc's did with this tool, we must understand Vodou as well as the social climate in New Orleans in which it and that activist emerged. Only then can we determine what Marie gained from or gave to her faith. Besides that, one cannot truly understand a famous leader of any faith without understanding the faith over which she reigned.

Chapter 4: What is Vodou?

Just a Word

My research shows that Marie LaVeaux was a humane and powerful leader—an outspoken healer whose power and charisma not only unified diverse factions of Vodou, but protected it from annihilation through the time of the Civil War. However, that is not the way LaVeaux is usually perceived. Often her detractors describe her work and her religion as an eclectic mix. Certainly she has rarely been acknowledged for the effective, creative model for social change that she built upon her faith and passed (circa 1850) to Mary Ellen Pleasant. My research also shows that the model and her faith were inseparable. So, the questions become, "What was Vodou in LaVeaux's time, and what did she gain from it and give to it? Did the religion sanction her and others to employ it socially as they did? Without daring to speak for Vodou or its related African/Diaspora faiths, this chapter and the next present answers to these questions based on my research and experience of these faiths. To facilitate review or scanning, I have highlighted key tenets of Vodou in tables. These chapters will reveal the continuity of worldview, process, and leadership that, I believe, enabled Vodou to serve as a "heritage of power" -- the basis of a model for social leveraging -- that Marie LaVeaux could pass to Mary Ellen Pleasant.

Vodou Is!!—Is not!!!

In the early part of this century Webster's dictionary defined Vodou in purely pejorative terms (Touchstone:1976). As late as the 1970's

Touissent Dessosier of New York called it, in essence, an amalgam of imagination (Desossiers 1970:35-39). Others have labeled it "additive or syncretic"—a faith that absorbs the ways of others without a consistent core of its own (Desmangles 1992). Even Harold Courlander, who once extolled Vodou as a true religion that creates order in chaos, called turn-of-the-century New Orleans Vodou medieval and European (Courlander 1976:50; Galembo 1998:xvi). Literary figure, Lafcadio Hearn and other scholars have agreed, citing elements of Catholicism, freemasonry, and German folklore, among other things, as influences (Long 7/98; Deren 1972; Herskovits 1972). What of these opinions? Even if they describe Vodou of the turn of the century, do they describe the religious heritage that inspired Marie LaVeaux?

Some writers say no because they feel that LaVeaux unified and inspired Vodou and that she, a devout, charismatic Catholic "turned bad," carried a true religion into a savage cult due to an inner "call of the wild" (LeBlanc: undated). They thereby denounce Vodou as having any part in inspiring her work, while applauding the worker. Many also report that she later renounced that cult for her "original" religion (The Daily States 6/17/81).

Some scholars disagree with both groups cited above. Author-practitioner/transpersonal psychologist Luisah Teish, Ph.D., argues that Vodou has endured hardship and diverse influences, but has maintained a contiguous African character with distinct beliefs (tenets), which unify it (Teish 1985:111). Ina Fandrich, the foremost LaVeaux scholar, concurs,

It is not the African heritage of Marie LaVeaux's activities and convictions, i.e., her involvement in the Voodoo religion that needs to be purged, but the racist, derogatory assumptions attached to these African cultural forms. For in my view, it is precisely the beauty, strength, and wisdom of LaVeaux's African cultural capital that enabled her to be who she was and what she stood for—the charismatic leader and key representative of New Orleanean Voodoo (Fandrich dissertation 1994).

Are these scholars correct? Is there a "beauty, strength, and wisdom" of Vodou —a "cultural capital" that was available for LaVeaux to draw upon in her work? Certainly, to many scholars (Desmangles 1992; Teish 1985, Fandrich 1994), Vodou is not the practice of evil hexes and spells depicted in the horror movies of the 1930's, 40's, and 50's, but rather an earth-centered (shamanistic) religion.

They do not deny that, after LaVeaux's death, Vodou in New Orleans sustained many disparate influences or that one offshoot, termed Hoodoo, is little more than secular magic. Nor do they deny the effect that European magic or the so-called 19th century hoodoo magicians like Dr. John or Dr. Yah Yah had on early New Orleans Vodou (Asbury 1938:258-60; Haskins 1992:87; Fandrich 1994:200). They rather assert that the questions to be answered are "What was the Vodou of Marie LaVeaux's time, and What heritage did she receive despite later changes in Vodou by the turn of the century? Did the work of the so-called magicians also grow out of African religion? Is dismissal of the Vodou faith as a collection of purely syncretic (accumulative) cults accurate, or is it simply a faulty way of looking at the normal process of adaptation that any transplanted faith undergoes?" (Brandon 1993: 180-184; Galembo/Fleurant 1998:iv-xviii; Brown 1991). Clearly, if the assenters are correct, then one must be able to find continuity and power in the faith despite its many additions and adaptations—enough continuity to have motivated both Pleasant and LaVeaux. And if this work is to assert with authority that Vodou did inspire the successes of both LaVeaux and Pleasant, it must answer these questions.

Meaning 1: Spirit Forces

Voodoo, Vodoun, or Vodou (a spelling currently preferred by many scholars) is a New-World, Diaspora faith that combines the religious traditions of West, North Atlantic, and West Central Africa with elements of other faiths. The word is derived from vodun (sometimes spelled vodu) in the Fon language of the Ewe/Fon people, who once lived in what is called old Dahomey, West Africa. Maps have changed drastically, but the home of the Fon is now Benin (Hurbon 1995). The Fon who influenced Vodou most were the Gbe speaking group, who held religious ties to the Yoruba of what is now Nigeria (Hall 1998:7; Geggus 1991, data section:12).

The first meaning of Vodou is "spirit forces." Its root word, Vodun, is the Fon name for worshipful, spirit beings or forces (primal divinities, later ones, and elevated ancestors). The word Vodun has two roots, vo and dun/du (Blier 1995), and, although all of Vodou is not Fon, examining the Fon-based name for the faith can reveal its focus and continuity. Thus, three meanings of Vodun will be examined here—1) divine spirit- (or spirit-force) beings, 2) that which comes after divination, and 3) that which is drawn to bring cooling, or peace (Blier 1995:38-40).

Forces in Common

The first meaning, spirit-force beings (or divinities), the most well-known of the three, reveals the focus of Vodou. Researchers and practitioners alike agree that, in Vodou and other African/Diaspora faiths, supernatural or divine forces or beings (known as Lwa/Loa) are entreated, along with ancestor spirits, to help devotees (vodouisants) live in harmony with the laws of the creator (Atanda lecture 11/4/1998; Somé 1997:11; Montenegro 1998:6; Teish 1985).

This belief in divine spirit-force beings originated in Africa and formed an area of continuity amongst African cultural groups long before New-World Vodou was formed. It follows, therefore, that some concepts in Africa that have been described as originating or evolving in Vodou simply reflect views always held in common amongst its diverse African constituents. For example, all believe that the divine spirit-force beings were ordained as helpers (intermediaries) by one Supreme Being (Bondye—the great God—in New Orleans and Haitian Vodou). He is the almighty Creator, the basis of all things (Awolalu 1996:1, 5). This one God assigned these helper-beings to various heavenly and earthly dominions from which they were to help run the creation and to assist mankind.

In New-World Vodou, many of these forces known in Africa were simply adopted or combined. For example, the spirit being to whom LaVeaux was ceremonially wedded is related to Danbala Wedo, or Dambada Hwedo (of Whydah, Benin). This being manifests there as a python and is always related to Ayida (Aido, Ayedo) Wedo, a similar being, depicted as a snake, who resides under the sea. One of the two

45

(most often Danbala) is also called the rainbow serpent. In oral scripture, either Danbala or his partner Ayida (varying by place and story) is also called "the most ancient one" because, as Fon oral tradition says, he was used by the Creator to help form the creation. Danbala was later called Papa Danbala in Haiti, and in some places is equated with the Creator because of his elder status. One Vodou song says of him, "Tu vje" (vieux)—You are old.

However, since all were related to a snake and regarded similarly, Damballah, Ayida, and Papa were easily equated in Vodou with the rainbow-serpent or ancient-serpent types of the Kongo (Mbumba Luango and Nzambi, respectively) and the Yoruba's Osumare. Combined, they became New Orleans' (and LaVeaux's) Damballah/Li Grand Zombi (Geggus 1991:27; Fandrich 1994). Such combinations were effortless because one group recognized the others' divinities as similar to their own in concept and lore.

One traditional Yoruba account, which greatly influenced the Fon, says that Osumare (Dambala-wedo) as the da (life force), was sent from the heavens (white clouds) to deliver God's covenant of life to mankind (Fatunmbi 1991: 84, 85; Brown 1991:13). In Haiti, he joined his counterpart, Ayida Wedo whom the most high God (Oludumare/Bondye) placed beneath the sea to hold up the earth (Herskovits, 1958:135). This union of two serpent life-force beings, which is recounted in many African cultural groups, always allows the pair to link sky and sea, rendering the earth a seamless whole. The Fon/Kongo composite, Damballah/Zombi of LaVeaux, embodied that lore too, manifesting as vibrational force (Fandrich 1994:210, 211; Metraux 1972:39; Geggus data:13)

In old Dahomey the home of the Fon people, these two primal spirit beings represent creation—the founding ancestors of that nation; in Haiti, the beginning of life (fertility). All relate to the life force (Da) or to the creations brought about by it (Brown 1991:273-276,312; Galembo/ Gerdes Fleurant 1998: xxi, xxii). Moreover, in all myths about them, this "super-serpent" team always fuses the earth and sea, just as the life force unites all life. Stories, gender, names, and ritual categories for these beings may vary somewhat by cultural group and place, but the fundamental concept of them remains throughout West, West Coastal, and West Central Africa, Cuba, Haiti, Brazil, and the United States (Courlander 1960:27). Related concepts today are the medical helix and DNA—that tool of the Creator that defines and unites all life—old indeed!

The same is true of other Lwa of the faith (Atanda lecture 11/1998). Among them, for example, one spirit (whether he is called Esu, Elegbara, Elegba petwo, Atibon 'Legba, or Papa 'Legba), is always regarded as a trickster, linguist of all spirits, and the doorkeeper between heaven and earth. He is clever and childlike in his need for gratification and knowledge. Like a teen, he tests things out, but always guards and opens the intersection between heaven and earth (the door to ritual), between the astral and the earthly spirit bodies (gros and petit bon ange), or between mankind and Spirit (Lwa and ancestors). A messenger, he always ferries messages to and from humans to other Spirit-force beings, especially to Fá, the Yoruba divinity of fate and divination (also called Orunmila) whom legend says was sent to restore order amongst the first spirit-force beings (Herskovits 1958:37-39; Atanda lecture 1998; Owolalu 1996:23).

Another primary spirit force called Erzili (named for the Azili river of Benin) mediates between fate and the other Lwa (Atanda lecture 1998). The wife of fate, she distributes order and wealth in the form of divination, sweetness, and progeny. She is called Oshun in Nigeria (Galembo 1998; Fatunmbi 1991:112). By either name and many others she is always associated with cool, cleansing fresh water and, like the honey bee, with aspects of love, sweetness, and fertilization (Desmangles 1992:10; Maes Valdez interview 1998). She does, however, have other aspects, some of which, as testament to migrations and interaction, occur throughout West Central Africa (Courlander 1960:27).

Many other primary forces are held in common amongst constituents of Vodou—

- The oceans' force—Agwe Twoyo/Olokun
- The earth's force—Azaka/Orisa Oko, etc.
- Iron's forces and products—tools, defense, and justice—called Ogou Feray, Ogun/Gu, etc.
- Fire's force (thunder and lightning) for strength and cleansing—Sango, Chango, Sogbo, Eshango, etc.
- The wind's forces as storms, death, and change—Oya, Bade, Baron Samedi, etc. and
- The force of balance through herbs, medicine, and magic—Osain/Osanyin

After these, the list of names grows and varies according to place—the basic concept for each divine being remaining similar in old-world (African) and Diaspora traditions, such as Ifá, Candomblé, Santeria, and Lucumí (Abimbola 1997a: 33, 106; 1997b:13, Hurbon 1995:72-79; Metraux 1972:88-91:Fatunmbi 1991:108-111; 1992:8). Thus, regarding what is worshipped, Vodou and its related faiths have long been unified around the belief that divine spirit intermediaries occur in a hierarchy below one Supreme Being.

Whether this God be called Bondye, Mawu, Olodumare, etc., God is always available through "His" Lwa ambassadors (Brandon 1993:13; Desmangles 1992:6; Fatunmbi interview 1998). Some of these ambassadors even took up residence in the earth's crust and elements after completing the creation assignments given them by the Creator. So, both their nearness and "charter" allow them, when entreated properly, to assist mankind (Desmangles 1992:5; Maes Valdez 1998) in living harmoniously within God's laws, and such harmony is considered a fundamental goal of life.

Most Africans believe that no one knows all of the divine forces (Lwa), but that they do not change because humans have yet to discover them. Accordingly, long ago, as Africans moved from one environment to another, they openly respected the "divine spirit-beings" of new places, and they carried that habit to the New World as vodouisants (worshippers). One unifying belief is that God's helpers for mankind are to be propitiated for their assistance wherever they are found. These divine spirit beings resemble the devas and devatas (divinities/ luminaries) in Hinduism, the spirits of the four directions and others of Native Americans, and the saints, archangels, and angels of Catholicism. This is perhaps one reason that elements of the latter two faiths were so easily incorporated into New-world Vodou (Brandon 1993:18; Bibbs lecture 1997).

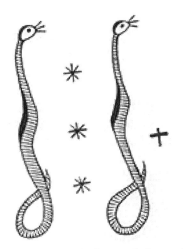

Artist's vèvè (symbol) for Danbala/Ayida Wedo

In New Orleans, diverse cultures (Senegambian, Mandinga, Bambara, Bakongo, Nago, Fon) held basic tenets regarding these worshipful forces and ancestor spirits in common along with a common need for constant communion with them (Somé 1997). Their appreciation of the omnipresence of the Divine spirit-beings (as either helpers or manifestations of the creator) produced clear reasons for accommodating them and their practices wherever found.

Forging Connections

Possession

In the search for unity amidst the diversity of Vodou, one finds also that devotees of African/Diaspora faiths all interact with Spirit directly. The constituents of Vodou all came from religions of spiritual inspiration rather than dogma—that is, from religions in which spirit forces interact with humans as part of normal religious practice as opposed to those in which that no longer regularly occurs as part of normal religious practice. Thus, in Vodou and its related faiths, divine spirit-beings regularly attend the praise ceremonies and the rituals that humans hold in their honor. The means of Spirit's arrival differs from group to group, but the principles of their arrival remain similar, possibly due to the constant exchange of ideas that occurred throughout Western, West Coastal, and Central Africa from the 2nd to the 19th centuries (Brandon 1993:20-27).

Within ceremony, forces always arrive through a conduit, such as an X (a symbol of communication between heaven and earth), an incantation, a designated post, a tree, or a snake (Nevadomsky: 1984: 191). Thus, LaVeaux held her python, a conduit called Li Grand Zombi (Damballah), as perhaps Moses held the Rod of Aaron, which became a snake before Pharaoh. Priests of Vodou (oungans) or priestesses (mambos) often employ conduits (ibid: 1991). During ritual, a pole in the temple (poteau mitan) serves as a conduit tree for spirits and messages between heaven and earth. In ceremony, the spirits also descend through that pole to priests or priestesses (houngans or mambos), who deliver their messages and healing to the group.

As Moses did, a Vodou priest or priestess usually serves as medium for direct, divine interventions, meant for attendees of the ceremony. For these reasons, in New Orleans, even today, LaVeaux's name is often associated with that of Moses (Millan interview 6/98). However, unlike the great God, Jehovah, of Moses, the spirit-force message givers of Vodou enter the body of initiates and designated others in order to give their helpful messages and guided healings (Deren 1953:16). This is called being "ridden" by Lwa, or "spirit possession." Regarded as a great opportunity to aid the community and to serve Lwa, "possession" is considered an honor in Vodou (Desmangles 1992), and it occurs in all of the original African cultural groups that comprise the faith. Thus, the concept of religion as continuously informed by Spirit through possession serves as another unifier in the faith and survives in all forms of Vodou.

Elements and Force

To form Vodou, the largest nations represented in New Orleans—Kongolese, the Senegambian, and Fon, etc., (Hall 1998:8) merged their faiths. This melding can be discerned in elements of Vodou other than in the names of divine spirit-beings. For example, whereas the word "Vodou" comes from the Dahomey, the word Lwa comes from the Kongo (whose people are called Bantu/Bakongo/Kongo, etc.), and many songs and ceremonies carry Senegambian or Bambara words and ways (Fandrich 1994).

A non-African element was also added to Vodou, but this one came by force. In New Orleans, as in Haiti, where slavery was prevalent, the laws of French and Spanish slave masters forced African slaves and their mulatto offspring to become Catholic, forcing them to practice the old ways in adaptive form. One could say that Lwa had to be camouflaged for safekeeping behind the ritual and saints of Catholicism. This combined African faith with a Catholic overlay became the core of what is called "Vodou." Said author and priest of Orunmila (Awo) Fa'lokun Fatunmbi,

The Black Codes, [French Laws followed by Spanish ones] mandated that slaves become Catholic. In some places they prohibited anything recognized as African practice, on pain of death. So, if camouflaging their practices or ordering them differently in ceremony protected the people, naturally they did that.

Later Black Codes under American rule would intensify the persecution, and in response, to preserve their new faith, the slaves "did that"—They performed Lwa feast days on Christian holy days, placed Catholic and African implements side by side on their altars or in sacred spaces (peristils), and represented them with the portraits of saints. Lwa were thus knowingly and secretly associated with (hidden behind) Saint names. Damballah, for example, was associated with St. Patrick because of that saint's depiction with the snakes of Ireland (Desmangles 1992:11). Vodouisants even added to ceremony their own symbolic Catholic priest (called "the bush priest") to represent the Church's teachings and ritual for Bondye (Bon dieux, the most high God), whom their faiths also acknowledged (ibid 1992:9). Thus, whereas a shared concept of Lwa facilitated the melding of the faiths of diverse African cultural groups in the New World, the need for safety proved a very strong impetus for the so called "syncretic" (additive or accumulative) practices of Vodou with the Catholic faith.

---

* see also MacDonald et al 1979:14

Chapter 5. Heritage of Power

Spirit Groupings

Beneath this protective camouflage, however, was order. In Haiti and New Orleans, where Vodou flourished, Vodou spirits and their rites were grouped into three categories (called nanchons), largely according to the cultural origin of participant groups. They were (and still are) called Rada, Kongo, and Kreyol—

1. Rada Rites—the major rites of Haitian, and later New Orleans, Vodou—belong to the original, African participant groups of the faith. The word rada stands for the town of Arada in Dahomey and therefore is also used to refer solely to the Fon constituents of Vodou (Metraux 1972:39, 86). There are, however, various interpretations of the meaning of the name, "Guinean/Guinen," which is also used both to refer to Fon or Nigerian Lwa and to refer to the entire group of original West African constituents of Vodou (ibid:87). Some stress that it refers to a mythical, not the actual, place—symbolizing a far-away homeland, which has been lost forever. Others say that it refers to a Valhalla-type place—the original home of the Fon divine spirit-beings (Vodun) (Hurbon, 1995:69). The spirit-beings of the Rada group, known also as the original spirits, dominate the faith and are regarded as "cool," benevolent, or helpful.

2. Kongo (Petwo) Rites are those that belong primarily to the West-Central-African spirit forces of the Kongo (The Democratic Republic of the Kongo as of 1960). In ancient times, the Bantu/Buntu people of this area migrated from Northwest, coastal Africa, through Yorubaland to Central and Southern African (especially the Kongo and Angola), so they are actually related to the Rada/Guinean groups (McEvedy 1995:32). However, in adapting to their new Central-African environment (here generally called Kongo or Angolan), they developed many warrior and hunting groups and a reliance on protective, "magical" practices, such as those used today in Quimbanda or those from the Kongo's Mayombre region (Montenegro, 1998:6).

In New Orleans, many Kongo ways, such as the protective/healing divination effigies called nkisi or nganga (holy ones) should have influenced LaVeaux's use of healing/charm effigies due to the large Kongolese presence there (Hall data 1998). However, the Central-Africans traveled in Africa, sharing such protective practices, so many were common throughout Western and Coastal Africa long before Diaspora faiths like Vodou, Quimbanda, or Palo Mayombre took hold in the New-World(Fatunmbi interviews 1998). Used generally for retaliation or defense and regarded as aggressive, unpredictable, or "hot," the petwo/Kongo spirit forces are less popular than the rada, but considered necessary for protection (Hurbon 1995:71), albeit risky to deal with. These "Lwa," such as Pomba Gira in Quimbanda or Palo, can exact penalties if not properly propitiated (Metraux 1972:88-89; Montenegro 1998:7; Hurbon 1995:82). Nevertheless, their rites, many born of cries for freedom, greatly enriched the ability of vodouisants (Vodou devotees) to protect themselves from harm, especially during enslavement in the New World (Montenegro 1998:6).

3. Creole/Kreyol Rites—As the word suggests, Kreyol rites are those that represent a variety of other spirits—old and newly discovered—many of whom function across groupings. Native American spirits/rites and others, such as Damballah (Nzambi in the Kongo) and Ayida Wedo (Mbumba in KiKongo), often considered rada, are also sometimes placed in this grouping. Those of the African constituents who were in the minority also fell here (Hurbon 1995:71; Desmangles 1992; Courlander 1960:27).

Some spirit forces sit in one group with one name and simply take a modified name (and a slightly different character) in another group. These are said by some to be separate members of one spirit family but by others to be aspects of the same force. For example, the moody, luxury-loving, rada Erzili Freda or the Fon Erzili Wedo, becomes the strong, protective, petwo Erzili Dantor, and there are Legba rada and petwo, etc. Rather than being indicative of confusion, this similar nomenclature with variation is strong testament to the continuity of belief that is held amongst even the most disparate groups in Vodou—

Yoruba and Kongolese, for example.

Catholic overlay plus these three categories of practice thus outline the diverse religious heritage that LaVeaux received. Her movements in possession might have looked Fon (Hurbon 1995:142) but the name that she often used for her primary spirit force (Li Grand Zombi) was derived from the Kongolese. West Africa's strong belief in Spirit communication and guidance through divination combined in her with the Bakongo's equally strong belief in the manipulation of natural forces for protection (protective magic). Marie probably used many Senegalese and Native American healing practices as well and certainly employed her favorite Catholic saints as part of her work. Nations, ceremony, and diverse spirit beings united freely around and within Marie LaVeaux.

Tenets of the Faith

There were thus beliefs in common (tenets) shared in Africa by all constituents, and there were also core practices. For example, special rite groupings across nanchons were usually formed for ceremony according to divination (systems of spirit communication). In fact, one reason that Fon spirit beings and ways eventually dominated New Orleans Vodou as they had earlier in Haiti (Geggus data article: 11-13) might have been the very ordered system of divination, which the Yoruba/Fon brought with them (Courlander1960:29).

Basic Tenets #1

As seen, African constituents of Vodou, whether Coastal, West, or West-Central African (Courlander 1960:27; Hall 1998) already possessed common tenets. These included

1. The belief in one Supreme Being (God) as orderer of the Universe

2. The goal of following God's laws through constant communion via God's designated spirit-beings and ancestor spirits (Somé 1997:52, 53; Atanda lecture 1998)

3. The belief in propitiating and praising Lwa, who constantly inform ceremony, and in adopting their ways and principles wherever found to affect mankind's destiny and to ward off evil—but not usually to conjure it (Montenegro 1998:6)

4. The belief in adapting to new environments harmoniously so as to maintain the equipoise that allows each devotee to achieve his/her highest destiny

---

All acquisitions by Vodou from other faiths are usually a direct result of one of these tenets. By propitiating and incorporating the ways of Lwa where they are found, vodouisants achieve one of their major life goals—adapting to new environments harmoniously (Fatunmbi 1998). Vodou, when viewed through its tenets, appears less random and less eclectic/syncretic than if viewed through its acquisitions alone (Brandon 1993: 176-80; Abimbola 1997). Spirit usually guides all such acquisitions, even if it conforms to one or more of these basic tenets, through divination. It is the double-check build into the system.

Meaning 2: Divination

The second derivative meaning of the word "vodun" is "that which follows/comes after divination." Divination is a practice (which can be part of any religion) in which a practitioner employs implements to contact Spirit directly or to petition a particular oracle (body of wisdom) for guidance. All over Western, Coastal, and Central Africa (as in India, Bali, and the Diaspora) it is used in similar ways. The implements used for it, however, vary from group to group. Since almost every ritual or result, including healing formulations and sacrifices, is determined by divination, this second meaning of vodun refers to the entire body of that practice and its results in the religion and its related faiths.

The second meaning comes about in this way: This time, the first syllable (vo) is said to relate to the root word "vau"— "sacrifices, etc., that follow" (Blier 1995); the second syllable, from dun (Du) refers to the scriptural divination system of the Nigerian Yoruba cultural group called Odu Ifá. The Fon people of old Dahomey (now of Benin) adopted Odu Ifá for conflict resolution centuries before coming to the New World. The Fon call the Yoruba scriptural passages Du and their divination system Fá, respectively. Thus, the entire Ifá divination system is also called Dafá—meaning "to make divination" (Fatunmbi 1992). Many African/Diaspora groups use Dafá.

So, the second derived meaning highlights a practice that unifies the faith (Blier 1995:38-40). Dafá or some related system, still used in West and Central Africa, the US, and the Diaspora, is very pervasive. This system survived when others did not perhaps because of its organization and the way in which it is learned. So, during slavery, it was able to help meld diverse slave religions in parts of the Diaspora. Scholar George Brandon, in his treatise on Santeria, a Diaspora religion related to Vodou, called Dafá (Ifá divination) a "flickering light" amidst the New-World slave traditions—meaning a ray of knowledge/culture preserved to guide believers within the darkness of slavery. So the discussion of Dafá here will be used to represent divination in Vodou although many other forms are used, because the practice is important in the faith and because its assumptions and structure reveal another way in which LaVeaux's Vodou was unified. Also, a description of Dafá is useful to a discussion of the Fon/Yoruba influence in the faith, in revealing the importance and structure of many African divination (scriptural-communication) systems, and in demonstrating well the reverence with which all devotees regard these folklore-like scriptures.

Dafá (Ifá divination) is highly organized. Each section (Odu/Du) of this Nigerian (Yoruba/Nago) scripture has eight parts. Some written versions now exist, but traditionally (like the Hindu Vedas) Odu is rigorously and systematically memorized by Africans in childhood and tested by elders (Bascom 1991:7-11; Atanda interview 11/9/98). Thus Odu were not easy to corrupt during slavery even though versions varied somewhat from place to place. There are 16 primary and 256 derived Odu, which recount various problematic life situations/occurrences and their remedies/prescriptives. Some scholars, therefore, describe these Odu as experientially derived through rigorous inquiry (Brandon 1993); others describe them as patterns/remedies from Orisa—the name for the divine Spirit-Force beings whom the Yoruba serve (Abimbola 1997b; Bascom 1991). Because they are said to reveal and record the messages of these worshipful beings, those who use Ifá divination sometimes call its many Du (Odu) "the secretaries of God."

Used daily for communicating with Lwa, to locate and treat sorcery, to select charms, medicines, or groupings (escorte) of Lwa for rituals, divination, as a major decision-making tool, is a primary underpinning of Vodou—(Metraux 1972:305-322). Divination helps vodouisants decide what should or should not be done or acquired, but as a tool, remains undisturbed by the acquisitions or prescriptions it recommends just as Vodou itself remains undiluted by the divinatory tools or techniques it adds or borrows from other faiths. (Bascom 1991. Brandon 1993:1-27; Metraux 1972:170, 305-322). For example, in the 19th century, when the cards of Spiritism were introduced to Vodou as divining tools, they were still used within established African/Diaspora divinatory principles, thereby enriching, without disturbing the faith itself.

Unity of Practice

In practice, divination, a unifier in Diaspora faiths, follows a basic pattern, regardless of the tool employed: A priest (such as an oungan or mambo of Vodou) seeks guidance from Spirit for a petitioner—individual or group—through a divination tool—the Kongo's wigi board-like animal tables, Haiti's Gembo (shell on a string), the Yoruba/Fon cowries, kola nuts, or divination chain, or New Orleans' candle with tafia and rum. In response, the oracle defines the situation and helps prescribe actions, wisdom, or remedies to address it

(Courlander 1972:36).

Often, as in Dafá, the divination tool points to one relevant section of scripture (Spirit message) in an oracle, such as Ifá scripture, but it may simply call up internalized scripture or forge an actual connection between the diviner and a Spirit Force or ancestor spirit to locate a remedy. After that step, the initiate usually gives the remedy -- the messages or actions discerned in divination for the petitioner that will address the situation at hand. The messages may include scripture, proverbs, and stories, and the actions usually require some investment (sacrifice) from the petitioner. The divination portion of the problem-solving process then ends.

To receive the desired result, the petitioner next has to perform the action/s prescribed; sometimes the priest can perform them in his or her behalf. Such actions can include prayers, incantations, food offerings, rituals, baths, or life-force sacrifices (Maes Valdez interview 1998). Sometimes protective talismans (dolls, packets, garde corps, arrèté, gris gris, etc) are given to arrest the work of negative magicians (Courlander 1972:98-100). Actions successfully performed and accepted by Spirit are believed to elicit a favorable result. If not, more divination and ritual can be done.

Extreme Points of View

The continuity of belief and practice just shown indicates that those who regard Vodou as totally eclectic or diluted by its acquisitions from other faiths hold an extreme point of view, which seems not to understand or to disregard the continuity of basic African beliefs. The well-known scholar Melville Herskovits added another point about Vodou's so-called syncretism. Once when he asked priests of Dahomey why their prescriptions and interpretations for the same situation differed from village to village, they replied that their Divine spirit-beings (Vodun) reveal different aspects of the same message to different people. They said, in essence, that sacrifices given by Vodun (Lwa) to humans (directly or via divination) are potentially infinite in number and that records of those messages in scriptures are really terms negotiated with spirit in a given place, under given circumstances, at a given time. They, therefore, make room for new solutions and regard the religions of others as sacred and the messages from Spirit everywhere (in scripture or practice) as valid. This understanding in African religions encourages selective borrowing of solutions to life problems and elements of ceremony from anyone, anywhere if those things seem to meet a given need (Herskovits 1963:27, 179-190).

Tendering Respect

In Africa, accommodations of this sort are considered respectful. West Africans have always welcomed visitors. If the visitors proved helpful against adversaries (as did the Portuguese for the Fon in the 15th century), they honored such helpers in song, incorporated their goods and Lwa (their guides) selectively, employed elements of their ceremonies, and praised their attributes in verses for posterity. This was done to acquire the best that Lwa had to offer (McEvedy 1995:76; Nevadomsky: 188, 190). Western and Central Africans began doing this long before they traveled as slaves to the New World.

Accordingly, Africans in Haiti and New Orleans, although forced to become Catholic under the French (up to 1767) and Spanish (up to

1803), would probably have incorporated elements of Catholicism (the local faith) without being forced, to pay homage to its praiseworthy "spirit-beings" (Christ, Mary, the Saints and angels). Author/Awo Fa'Lokun Fatunmbi, one of the few Westerners initiated as a Babalawo (divining priest) in Ode Remo, an ancient seat of Ifá, explains that all West-African faiths stress adapting to the environment (Bascom 1991) and that the mandate to adapt to environment encourages accommodation above racial or cultural considerations. Said Awo Fatunmbi,

> *Much of African spirituality is practical advice and wisdom, leading to the manifestation of good health, strong family, and future progeny, so the criterion for pure exchange has always been practical—"what worked" to solve problems— not differences in language and customs or race.* (Fatunmbi interview 1998).

Wande Abimbola, Ph.D., the former Harvard and Boston University scholar who is the international spokesman for Yoruba diviners, agreed that the overall goal of all West African (rada) religions has always been to adapt to environment. To do so, they have always used whatever brings devotees a measure of peace and balance in what they see as an inherently conflict-ridden world (Abimbola 1997:33, 72). The tasks of incorporating the Lwa and ways of their "conquerors" and combining their various faiths to stave off annihilation and conflict in a new environment also helped form LaVeaux's unique, but cohesive, religious heritage.

Basic Tenets #2

From the discussion on continuity in Vodou, these tenets can be added—

1. that the goal of life is balanced living, which entails continuous conflict resolution and a constant balancing of opposites (light and darkness)

2. that it is, therefore, wise both to adapt harmoniously to new environments and their inhabitants and to incorporate the guidance of spirit everywhere

---

Expansive Belief

The West African belief that every religion tries to lead its devotees to happiness in the world also promotes their adoption of foreign practices, according to Professor Abimbola and scholar Joseph Nevadomsky, of the Centre for Social, Cultural, and Environmental Research at the University of Benin (Nevadomsky 1984:206; Abimbola 1997:33). In a recent interview well-known author/initiate Carlos Montenegro agreed, saying that Spirit is not racist and that the temple always sets aside cultural differences (Montenegro1998:7). Awo Fatunmbi summarized this view of the African/Diaspora faiths in this way—

All men and women universally look for the same things— health, money, and progeny. West Africans are taught culturally that it is proper to accommodate others and to pursue their faith humbly. (Fatunmbi interview 11/1998)

From that vantage point, Vodou's incorporation of the ways of others (so-called syncretism) results from inclusiveness and a largess of belief (Brandon 1993:176-80), and it matters little whether the source of the life remedies they select come from sources that are similar, related, or foreign, Catholic, African, European, or Kabalistic. Just as a pharmacy is enriched by the effective prescriptives that it gathers, Vodou is enriched by the effective practices it acquires in a quest to assist devotees. Moreover, if cognitive psychology is correct in saying that enlightenment comes out of human investigation that uses human experiences as fertilizer for growth, then a religion that seeks balance for its devotees through testing and incorporating diverse experiences and remedies, without sacrificing its own scripture or process, would appear to afford a reasonable way of achieving it (McBratney/Kegan unpublished thesis 1998:24).

Shared Worldview

Wande Abimbola added to this significantly by saying that the diverse West African people share many beliefs because they are really one people. History bears him out. Groups from the North Atlantic coast (Senegambia) to Central Africa (the Kongo/Angola) comprise the Niger-Congo language group (McEvedy 1995:32), and three primary West African cultural groups—the Yoruba, Fon, and Ewe—actually trace their lineage to three sibling princes. Moreover, prior to colonialism, African territories functioned more like neighboring corporations or related clans than today's city states (Brandon 1993; McEvedy 1995; Desmangles 1992; Farris Thompson 1984:16; Bascom 1991:3-8).

Examples of intermingling abound. Fon priests at one time

customarily traveled to Yorubaland to study Dafá (Abimbola 1997:86), and Fon stories say that Dafa came to them through diviners who traveled freely from Yorubaland. Yoruba scripture (Odu) makes reference to Islam, possibly as a result of the Senegambian Fulani warriors who interacted with them. All demonstrate that the creation of Vodou should not have been difficult and that its accumulative practices sit on a firm base that did not originate in the New-World.

Thus, New-World Vodou is similar to its predecessors, and since their tenets mandate dynamic adaptation to environment, their New-World sects do not deviate from the faith by following that mandate. (Brandon 1993; Abimbola 1997; McEvedy 1995). More importantly here, their ease in sharing new ideas and prescriptives shows that, over many centuries, these related, but well demarcated groups carried very similar world views and ways. These became the cohesive, heritage of power (the "cultural capital") that they brought with them to Vodou and to Marie LaVeaux. Scholar Ina Fandrich concurred when she wrote,

> *Their African heritage offered a set of striking similarities in terms of worldview, cultural and aesthetic norms, ...which in my view, became instrumental in the formation of New Orleans Voodoo* (Fandrich 1994: 69, 70).

A ritual flag for Esu, the spirit who represents the
crossroads of communication between heaven and earth—
Esu is common to many African/Diaspora traditions.
Photo by the author, flag by Ile Orunmila Oshun, Oakland

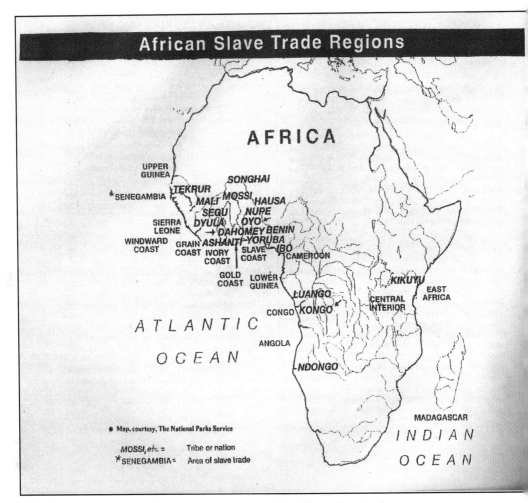

Map showing regions of the African Slave Trade

Chapter 6. Religion or Cult??

Nays and Yeas

Clearly, Vodou contained enough continuity in her time to have inspired and guided Marie LaVeaux in concept and in divination. Although that unity would have been enough to direct LaVeaux's work, was it sufficient to allow the faith to be called a religion rather than a cult? This work cannot really determine this issue definitively, but an in-depth discussion of it should prove useful in revealing the unity and creative mandates that guided Marie LaVeaux and, later, Mary Pleasant.

Some say Vodou is not a religion for three reasons—

1. It lacks continuity of leadership and purpose, even if its adherents do share some common views

2. Its regional acquisition of practices renders it far too eclectic and contradictory to be called a religion (Hurbon 1995:14; Courlander 1950), and

3. Its leaders, which are allowed to innovate freely on whim, distort and corrupt the faith too much to allow it that status (Asbury 1938 260).

In response, other scholars and practitioners say,

1. That, since its many of its predecessors and other Diaspora faiths are considered religions, a faith possessing the same elements must be considered a religion as well (Abimbola 1997).

2. That no living religion is exactly like that of its predecessors

3. That all adapt and change regionally as they respond to

new circumstances and visions of leadership (Brandon 1993).

4.   That the various sects of Vodou need agree no more than the highly distinct sects of Christianity (Abimbola 1997a),

5.   That Vodou possesses the same basic elements found in all religions—belief in divinity, a hierarchical priestly body and consistent leadership, a society of the faithful, temples, altars, ceremonies with clear elements, and a means of transmitting scripture (Price-Mars per Hurbon 1995:144; Abimbola 1997)

For these reasons, Vodou should be called a religion.

Seeing the Elephant

Those who feel that they "see" the faith clearly regard the dissenters as like the three blind men in an old Hindu fable—Three blind men examined the same elephant, but each described him differently. How could this be? All touched him, but one described him as long and thin like a long hose, the other as flat and rough like a course wall, and the third, like a chord with hairs at the end. All, equally blind, described the same elephant, but from his own point of view—trunk, side, or tail—and no one saw the whole.

Scholar-practitioners of Vodou and related faiths say that those who view Vodou from the vantage point of their own dogma-based religions are unable properly to see (grasp) the whole of the Vodou faith—one that amends itself based on continuing mystic inspiration (Fatunmbi interview 1998; 1991:120 Deren 1953:17). They add further that only two questions need be answered to determine whether

LaVeaux's Vodou was a religion, despite what might have happened to the faith after her time. They are—"What elements in common with other religions did Vodou possess in LaVeaux's time?" and "What, if anything, guided LaVeaux's creative use of her faith?" Examining these questions will reveal continuity of leadership and initiation and other common elements of LaVeaux's Vodou that made it a religion and how those things determined the course of her work.

Continuity

In LaVeaux's time the convergence of several factors brought continuity to the faith. However, the elements it holds in common with all religions—a priestly lineage, clear initiation practices, and ordered ceremony—allow it to qualify to be called a religion rather than a cult. (Bibbs 1997; Hurbon 1995:144)

Haitian Priests

Even though the Kongolese and Senegambians dominated New Orleans Vodou in number during LaVeaux's formative years, several factors converged to allow Fon (rada) Lwa and practices to dominate content in the faith. First, in the early 1800's, Haitian fpc's (Marie's social group), entered New Orleans in large numbers. In 1819 she even married one of them. Some reports say that 5,000 Haitian fpc's immigrated into New Orleans after the Santo Domingo (Haitian) revolution seeking prosperity after their country had been ravaged by war. As mentioned earlier, fpc's soon became 18% of the City's total population. Many of them were very European in behavior and staunch Catholics (MacDonald/Davis 1979; Hall 1998; Geggus 1991); however, after Catholic priests had fled the island during the early part of the Haitian revolution, many Haitians began practicing both vodou and Catholicism—serving spirits for everyday life and worshipping in church as part of their religious practice.

The Haitian fpc initiates who came to New Orleans brought with them the rada (Fon/Nago) context that dominates Haitian Vodou. These initiates, who, along with mulattos and maroons (escaped slaves), dominated the priesthood of Vodou in Haiti, often possessed both education and leadership skills, so they soon led the priesthood of New Orleans Vodou (Asbury1938:255; MacDonald 1991:22). MacDonald 1991:22). Many lived amongst and intermarried with the fpc's of Marie's group. Marie studied with one, and they met near Marie's home. Thus, they should have influenced Marie's growth in and perception of the faith. Since they shared her basic beliefs, their practices should have complemented her earlier Sengalese-Congolese training.

Special Convergence

In addition, the period between 1807 and 1830, brought a fortunate convergence that influenced Vodou in New Orleans. The fall of the Benin and Yoruba Oyo empires brought large numbers of homogenous groups of Fon/Yoruba slaves from Africa via the Caribbean, giving the greatly increased slave population a propensity towards the rada version of Vodou.

While these new freeborn priests and new rada-oriented slaves were entering, two other favorable things occurred. Circa 1805 the Americans, who had taken over Louisiana, passed an ordinance that allowed slaves to socialize and congregate for the first time (Asbury:1938:239, 240).

These allowed vodouisants to worship and to dance in public on the weekends. So, Vodou, in public and in private, began to flourish in New Orleans, a primary gathering place.

The Kongo influence would have given LaVeaux certain forms of twirling, spinning, or shaking movements in dance, devotion towards Nzambi (an ancient Kongo snake Lwa), knowledge of the making and selling of healing or protective effigies or charms, and the ability to do certain types of readings. Fon influence would have encouraged certain tenets of divination and scriptural mandate, a different form of initiation, and the use of the python in worship—the melding of Damballah and Ayida Wedo with the BaKongo Nzambi. These elements can, in fact, be discerned in some descriptions of LaVeaux's ceremonies (Fandrich 1994:210-211; LWP 25). For example, in ceremony LaVeaux used movements still associated with possession by Danbala Wedo in Benin, and she often wore blue at those times. In Haiti blue is the color for the water Lwa Damballah's first and second brides, Ayida Wedo and Erzili (Metraux 1972:167; Hurbon 1995:142). Marie LaVeaux thereby embodied the brides of Damballah in those ceremonies.

So, on Saturday's and Sundays in the old Brickyard on Dumaine St. (and later in Congo, or Circus Square), just a stone's throw away from Marie's home, vodouisants celebrated rare moments of freedom and communion with their homeland in ritual, dance, and song, albeit under the watchful eye of the police. The result in New Orleans was a religious movement, a social force, and a business all in one. Within that setting, Marie ascended her throne.

This scenario does not deny the earlier African influences that persisted and enriched all aspects of New Orleans Vodou. However, it does assert that a fresh influence of Fon/Yoruba scriptural leadership, thought, and practice entered New Orleans Vodou to render the religion that Marie encountered in her formative years more unified than has usually been reported and certainly more unified than it became in the late nineteenth century. (MacDonald et al 1991: 11-14; Abimbola 1997:84, 98-106; Asbury 1938:239-242; Hurbon 1995:16,21).

Backed by historical fact, research, and to some extent, records, these facts challenge the assertions of those who say that Vodou held no cohesive base of leadership or scriptural continuity during LaVeaux's time (Brandon 1993:13; MacDonald 1991:11; Hall, 1998; Geggus 1991:11).

Priestly Lineage

Most importantly, Vodou possesses the three elements that define all religions—a priestly lineage, clear initiation practices, and ordered ceremony. With rare exceptions, priests of Vodou are initiated by someone and so have a priestly lineage, despite the diversity of the faith, and so did Marie LaVeaux. One of the earliest Vodou queen's in New Orleans was named Sanité Dédé (pronounced San-ee-tay Day-day). Dédé, a quadroon, was a Haitian (rada-oriented) free woman of color—one of the immigrants mentioned above. By day, she merely sold sweet meats in Jackson Square, but otherwise, she was one of New Orleans' most enduring Vodou queens (Metraux, Geggus 1991:11-13; Asbury 1938:239-260; Kelley interview 1996). Legend says that she taught another queen named Marie Saloppé, who later rivaled her, and that queen Saloppé, in addition to a Senegalese priest, taught Marie LaVeaux (Tallant 1991). There is no proof of this, but if true, this legend confirms

Marie LaVeaux's rada-oriented training as it makes her part of Dede's priestly lineage (Asbury 1938:260; Kelly interview 1995; Tallant 1946). Vodou, thus, has the priestly lineage required of all religions.

Sanité Dédé, an early priestess (mambo) who influenced Marie LaVeaux
Courtesy, New Orleans Voodoo Museum, Brandi Kelley

Traditional Initiation

Whether or not the Saloppé legend is true, there can be no doubt that, to become priestess (then as now), Marie had to be initiated. And, if she were a disciple of a Haitian mambo, LaVeaux should have undergone an elaborate three-stage initiation (lavé têt, marriage, and couché) that bound her to the injunctions and practices of a mambo (Brown 1991; Fandrich 1994; Fatunmbi 1991:102-107). Initiations vary in Vodou, but with rare exception, all priests undergo one.

Ceremonial Progression

Vodou also has ordered ceremonies, some of which have elements that resemble those of other religions. In fact, before their exposure to the Church, many African ceremonies held elements similar to those of Catholicism. Yet, Vodou's indigenous and similar elements have often been mistaken for purely imitative ones. For example, in 1825 the opening of one of Sanité Dédé's ceremonies in the brickyard near LaVeaux's home was observed and later described in an account by a man who had attended as a child. The original report merely said that, to begin her ceremony, Dédé signaled to four initiates in a crescent formation, then made "cabalistic signs" and sprinkled liquid from a calabash over them while she muttered something softly (Ashbury1938:262). Later, one author, quoting this interview, suggested that this opening displayed Vodou's syncretism—use of Catholic and mystic elements in ceremony. The author's mistake was a common one.

However, some scholars, including Nigeria's Wande Abimbola, remind us that widespread in West-African, traditional ritual the same elements appear—processing, cleansing ritual space, employing "mystic symbols," and performing incantations. All were standard practice long before the soon-to-be Voduisants encountered Catholicism (Abimbola 1997:83; Bibbs lecture 10/27/1997; Brandon 1993, Somé 1997:68; Metraux 1972:159-191).

During mass the Catholic priest does process to his altar area in formation with altar attendants; he does make the sign of the cross (a mystic symbol), does mutter an invocation (prayer) after casting holy water while processing with his ritual items, and he does spread incense smoke over the crowd to cleanse the ritual space and congregation. The actions in many Yoruba rituals may differ in meaning from those of Catholicism, but the slaves observing the Catholic ritual would not have discerned that originally. What they saw seeemed similar.

In Vodun and other faiths, the ritual space and attendees are cleansed with herbs that are both burned and sprayed. A connection between man and spirit is then forged using liquid "spirits" (rum, etc.). A cross roads symbol (such as an X) is drawn in the air and represented symbolically elsewhere to provide a point of entry between the spirit realm and earth. Those forces are housed in pots/packets that have been placed on an altar. Incantations by the primary and attendant priests are performed to call Spirit to ceremony (Bibbs lecture, 1997).

This opening ceremonial progression--processing, cleansing ritual space, employing "mystic symbols," and performing incantations, which is common to many faiths, reinforces the standpoint of those who would call Vodou a religion and might explain the vodouisants' continuing affinity for Catholic ceremony. Perhaps such similarities between Vodou and Catholic practices also explain why in the 1990's in Haiti, when it was suggested that one of the primary Catholic elements in the Vodou ceremony be removed, vodouisants saw no reason to do so (Desmangles, 1992).

Vodou opening	Catholic opening
The vodou priest enters in formation with attendants	The Catholic priest enters in formation with attendants
The priest cleanses the space with herbal or tobacco smoke and sprays liquor as a cleansing and to establish communication with spirit	The priest cleanses the space with incense smoke and flings holy water as a cleansing
The priest and attendants salute the four directions	The priest makes the sign of the cross
The vodou priest invokes spirit	The Catholic priest speaks opening invocations and prayers to God
During ceremony, the priest facilitates wisdom-sharing in ceremony by praising Lwa, which includes responsive song	The Catholic and Lay priests share wisdom in ceremony through scripture and homily and responsive song

Similarities perceived between Catholic and Vodou ceremonial openings

Chapter 7: Creative Ways

Given that it meets the three criteria for all religions, Vodou should be called a religion even with what Haitian houngan Max Beauvoir calls the glue that is its inherent diversity (Gates film, 2011). The second major objection to calling Vodou a religion is that its oungans (priests), mambos (priestesses), and queens (great leaders), being autonomous, corrupt the faith by imposing their own imaginings upon it. Did LaVeaux simply impose her whims on her followers and the religion? Did she merely usurp the powers of the religion to effect her social agenda? Was LaVeaux's social use of her faith and the social model that she built upon it, traditionally mandated or her own personal creation? A look at the concepts of sacrifice, divine inspiration, initiation, and the proverb, along with the social conditions in New Orleans during LaVeaux's reign should answer these questions.

Sacrifice of Necessity

After divination of any kind a sacrifice (an offering of value to spirit) often results. Here the term sacrifice, common in most religions, should be explained because it has been distorted with reference to African religions, especially Vodou. Many in the Judeo-Christian tradition are familiar with biblical sacrifices, which involved offering God the first fruits of a crop or the best of a herd. As does Vodou, most traditions that offer life-force sacrifices do so in a "kosher" way—after divination accompanied by prayer (Abimbola 1997). However, in no religion is life-force offering regarded as the only form of sacrifice. All, including

African/Diaspora faiths, agree that these vary with the circumstance and that there can be alternatives even when life-force offerings are ordained. In those cases the attitude of the giver is the key to the effectiveness of the sacrifice.

Accordingly, one Yoruba proverb (part of Du) clearly states that Spirit (Lwa) will bless one who offers even water, if he or she does so with sincerity (Fatunmbi 1994), a proper sacrifice being one prescribed and an alternative being one that spirit has agreed to accept as a substitute. This proverb, interpreted traditionally, says that an alternative sacrifice must simply be seen as necessary and rendered with sincerity. Thus, vodouisants need not always offer what is prescribed traditionally.

As mentioned, in Vodou, unlike some related faiths, the primary message receivers are usually initiates, who are tempered to lead others and to receive divine energies. The devotees, therefore, revere their priests as "consecrated (holy) people," and they expect the chief initiate —their Yeye (venerable/beloved elder) queen—to be a conduit for innovation and divine inspiration. This is a reason that Vodou queens have always been allowed to innovate freely.

Given this expectation, however, whatever insights LaVeaux received from Damballah (Li Grand Zombi) as prescriptive for her people, she would have felt impelled to share whether they involved the use of prayer or guinea peppers. Whatever calling or special power (juju) she received from spirit, she would have implemented, and her devotees would have welcomed. The validity of this level of respect in the faith is hard for some scholars and others outside of the tradition to accept, and yet the holy "man" (or woman) as a consecrated being, open to inspiration, is a concept common to all religions, especially in Catholicism.

Mystic Inspiration

One of the primary elements (and tenets) of Vodou and its related faiths is mystic inspiration—The receipt of actual messages from spirit. In divination, whether the implement used be cowries or a deck of cards, whether the message be read from Odu or given directly through the initiate, the prescriptive, when given, is considered valid because the true oracle is the diviner (oungan or mambo). By definition, in Vodou, one who has been initiated is consecrated—holy in the sense of being "opened" to Spirit messages. The process of initiation is a three stage, rigorous one. Thus it matters little whether LaVeaux was exposed to a formal scripture during her training, because as an initiate, she would have received messages from Lwa and prescribed valid sacrifices (or prescriptives) based on mystic revelations and her own insights, and her method of divination. Every Vodou ceremony provides a space for mystic inspiration through direct Spirit messages (Drewal 1992:xix), and when spirits speak there, they also give directions that modify existing practices. Thus, mystic inspiration and messages and priestly consecration produce change and variety regularly in the religion.

Meaning 3: Finding Peace

However, even if initiates do not receive direct mandate through possession or divination, African scripture allows them (being aligned with Spirit in initiation) to employ their own insight for the good of the people. A third meaning of vodun highlights their mandate -- helping devotees achieve good character (balance and alignment with their highest destiny). This enables them to find some measure of peace in the world (Blier 1995; Abimbola 1997: 106-107; Maes Valdez 1998; Fatunmbi 1991). The syllables of vodun in this case mean "one draws water for rest." According to Benin scholars, "for rest" here means "for cooling" -- that is, to find peace (Blier, 1995: 38-40). A priest must innovate to help vodousiants achieve this peace -- the primary goal of Vodou and all related African/Diaspora faiths. Du explains --

oniwa funfun—One with good character is guided by light (Fatunmbi 1994:1),

meaning -- one with good character is able to receive the highest guidance of Spirit. Vodou and its related religions believe that the key to finding peace is good character because to gain it one must learn to maintain balance ("cool-headedness" or itutu) in the world. This is also called having a cool head, or orí tùtú. Only one with a cool head is present in the moment to receive the highest guidance that Spirit has to offer in any given situation. So, only one with a cool head can receive the blessings (àshé) that any given situation has to bestow (Farris Thompson 1995:16).

In Vodou one might describe this type of equipoise (itùtú or orí tùtú) as the state of having the heavenly guardian-body of thoughts and feelings (gros bon ange) in alignment with the individual one (petit bon ange). The same concept is held in religions in other parts of the world as well. For example, the Hindus of India use the word Yoga for itutu (the balance of cool-headedness). Yoga is defined in their sacred scripture called The Bhagavad Gita as

Samatvam Yoga uchyate—"Equipoise is Yoga, it is said." In The Gita the Lord, represented by Krishna, says this to the main protagonist (the warrior Arjuna), who is seeking equipoise on the battlefield of life.

To complete the definition, Lord Krishna later adds, *Dukha samyoga viyogaha uchyate*—"It is said that Yoga (equipoise, or cool-headedness) is that which disjoins one from the joining with sorrow" (H.H. Swami Chinmayananda 1976; H.H. Swami Dayananda Saraswati 1988).

Therefore, it was LaVeaux's mandate as queen (as it is the mandate of every mambo) to do all within her power to bring peace ("cooling") to those in her community—to guide them towards good character, to protect them, and to encouraged balance.

Proverbs—Being Cool

Even if LaVeaux never encountered the saying from Odu mentioned above in its scriptural form—Oniwa funfun, she would have received the same mandate through proverbs. Proverbs embody the values of a society, and being short, are usually transmitted intact. In fact, in New Orleans, common lore, proverbs, and folklore have became so infused in the society at large that everyone, regardless of race, repeats and lives by them (Teish, 1998: interview; McDonald 1979:18; McGowan:108, 176-177). Proverbs, often scripturally based, are similar in all of the African cultures that comprise Vodou. Thus, were there no ceremony, no possession, no scriptural instruction, no traditional divination, the traditional wisdom of African proverbs would still have reached and guided the Vodou queen, enabling her scripturally to adapt religious practice to the needs of her people (Drewal 1992:4).

From this, one can glean the presence of guidance for any priest and the absence of a need to be guided by whim. For example, one proverb derived from Du says—

A pot that boils over puts out the flame. (Fatunmbi 1994:23),

meaning that one must keep a cool head (orí tùtú) to avoid self sabotage. This saying would most certainly have reached LaVeaux and been incorporated as a personal value. It has, in fact, become one of Africa's and the world's most famous sayings—the admonition for balance, "Be cool." Africans say it all the time. We all do, and in the context of a society, this saying implies the same meaning as the Odu verse.

Further, above achieving good character or having enough cool-headedness to maintain balance to make/receive the best of any situation (àshé), being cool also mandates individual variation and creativity. We say, "She's cool!" meaning "She's unique or creative." One who is " cool" is also considered able to be to behave innovatively (Osumare lecture 4/1998). Another clear message is that "cool" opposes rote conformity, which is insufficient when one wants to be artful. Accordingly, in all African-based cultures, set forms become merely a basis for improvisation (coolness) whether in singing, dancing, playing jazz, or in just expressing.

Those cultures demand that something be added or repeated with a little variation (critical difference)—that one "put ones stamp on anything" in order to make it artful—cool—something special (Drewal 1992:4). In religions they have the same expectation. Cool is always achieved within an established framework, just as one must be guided in varying music by the confines of the original melody. Unless (as permitted by the first proverb above) special circumstances prevail, the priest must be guided by the basic tenets of faith. Therefore, LaVeaux's mandate was to be cool—to maintain the basic beliefs of Vodou while making a unique contribution to it.

"Being cool" has also come to mean, by extension, looking smart and being clever (Drewal 1992:xv; Thompson 1973). Today, as in LaVeaux's time, the "cool aesthetic" pervades all of African and African-American religion, art, and culture (Osumare 1998). To be respected, therefore, a leader too must be considered artful—really cool; to hold power, a great leader therefore must be "cooler" than the rest. Thus, a great queen not only had to assimilate the mandate to adapt ceremony to her insights and environment as needed to bring peace to her people, but she had to earn her greatness by "leaving her mark" on the faith. She had to innovate.

Of course, we know that LaVeaux was New Orleans Vodou's greatest queen. Therefore her innovations within the frame of her injunctions were as expected—They brought pride, protection, and unity to her faith. From the power of her religious and cultural heritage, not eclecticism or whim, Marie LaVeaux brought a special creative vision to Vodou. For Marie, "being cool" meant using a bold, social-activist's form of Vodou to protect and inspire.

Initiation—Growing Up

One other belief would have impressed LaVeaux—the belief that becoming a priest is growing up in one's religion and culture (Somé

1994). This way of looking at initiation, which pervades all West and Central African traditional religions, should have provided the strongest mandate for her social work and innovations.

In these religions, as devotees grow up they are expected to grow spiritually and to assume increased responsibility in their community. The biggest of these steps in social, spiritual, and religious growth is marked by initiation. It is considered a personal empowerment or alignment with Spirit that enables one to achieve his or her highest potential (Somé 1995; Atanda lecture 1998). Initiation puts a person in alignment and communication with the Lwa that particularly guides that person, and so it is seen as a desirable step for anyone if divination approves it.

In fact, the Yoruba refer to initiation as placing a devotee "in the center of the divination tray," their divination tray being a two-dimensional representation of the universe or eternity and the center representing perfect balance (Awolalu 1996; Fatunmbi 1991). In Vodou to be aligned and fully opened to communication with the Lwa "on your head" or to be "wedded to" a given Lwa is to be opened to one's greatest personal power (àshé). The expectation is that, once Spirit sanctifies one in that way, he or she has a responsibility to guide and serve the community with that power (Maes Valdez interview 1998). It is "the bottom line" for any priestess. Becoming a mambo is a three-step process that can take time (Fandrich 1994), but to become a priest (mambo or hougan) is inherently to be prepared to give back much more than time to the community.

Further, to serve well, a mambo must be skilled, becoming adept in healing and spirit incantation, performing beneficent and protective rites and, perhaps, even midwifery. In short, said priestess Xochipala Maes Valdez in a recent radio interview, "An initiate must learn to do the right thing in the right way at the right time" (ibid 1998) for her community.

This, in effect, would have been LaVeaux's mandate whether her teacher was Senegalese or Haitian. Having learned well, she would have trusted herself to act in behalf of her people, and her people, however she defined them, would have trusted her. She certainly would have passed that mandate to Mary Pleasant (Teish interview 7/98). Becoming a priestess in these traditions does not separate one from family or livelihood and is not an end in itself. Rather it is a rite of passage. Functionally, the person is aligned (wedded) to the power of a given Lwa (spirit force) and is then expected to grow through that connection. The success of the priest in fulfilling the promise of that rite remains to be seen just as, after the marriage ceremony, the success of any marriage remains to be seen. We know LaVeaux fulfilled the promise of her wedding to Damballah far more creatively than anyone in New Orleans had done before her, ultimately earning the right to be called "the most powerful woman there is."

City in Turmoil – A Hell on Earth

As well, social and political factors forced Marie and her class, the fpc's, to become active socially or to use the religion to affect the society at large. Not the least of their worries was the horrid state of New Orleans by 1836, approximately at the time that Marie became queen. In the 19th-century French Quarter, free people of color did business, and many exhibited the design, style, and architecture that French education had afforded them. They provided goods and services for white Creoles and others. They also often displayed the pride of the freedom and the wealth that they had known before American rule. But, after the 1820's, under the firm and often hostile grip of the Americans, political retaliation against the former Creole regime, political corruption, and bias brought chaos to the City and all of its people. It also threatened the liberty of the free people of color.

Almost immediately upon taking control of New Orleans in 1803, American slaveholders opposed the free, landowning men and women of color, coveting their holdings and (with good reason) fearing their education, love of liberty, and the power of their Vodou rites. After the French Revolution, these fpc's in Haiti ("Affanchis"), filled with a love for liberty, had been suspected of inciting rebellion, and indeed, African Vodou rites had ejected Napoleon's forces during the revolution there. These factors brought increasing persecution and disenfranchisement to free people of color in New Orleans. Naturally, they resented it.

In addition, by 1836, those New Orleaneans who belonged to the so-called No Nothing Party, (as in We know nothing but the constitution) were in accord with the slaveholders. They brought violence to the streets, allowed ruffians to coerce the people, and created a corrupt police force with unfair jailing practices. By 1850, the time of the Fugitive Slave Law and the gold rush, the free people of color and their Creole relatives faced discomfort and extinction, along with their indigenous religion and their way of life (Haskins 1992:59).

The citizens, especially the Creoles and the fpc's reacted, not by becoming revolutionaries, but by becoming social activists. As the words of an old blues song say, "God bless the child who's got his own."

They therefore took some matters of their own social welfare into their own hands.

Adding insult to injury, the corrupt civic government, ignored the cries of the entire New Orleans citizenry by refusing to clean the filth and stagnant water from the gutters. The lack of sanitation brought plagues to the City and fear of the death that seemed to hover everywhere In fact the New Orleans Delta called the place, "A Hell on Earth" (Asbury 1938; Millan interview 1998).

This climate produced for New Orleaneans a need for pride and protection, a need for change and control in a world that seemed out of control. Unusual times called for unusual means. This desperate state of affairs brought many Creoles and white New Orleaneans to the doorstep of Marie LaVeaux for readings, spells, healing, and favors. The protection of the people—the duty of a priestess—was called for by the City at large. So, in addition to the mandate of her religious heritage, we might say that social chaos and bias gave sanction and birth to the work of Marie LaVeaux.

Photo presumed to be that of Marie LaVeaux,
courtesy, The Historic New Orleans Collection

Chapter 8: Moving On

Woman Power

We know that for any f.p.c, most of whom were born Catholic, Catholicism and Vodou simply co-existed and that each held a special place for the people. Vodou brought a sense of community to the people and cared for their daily needs. Membership in the church brought them privileges in the society at large and taught them about Bondyé—the most high God for whom Vodou offered less discourse and interaction. So it is today as well.

But for Marie, who loved the Church, Catholicism also offered new spirit forces to revere. Perhaps she saw the priests as interpreters of those New-World Lwa because she often worked with them to heal the sick or to comfort the imprisoned. Certainly she respected them, but she could not become a Catholic priest, and unlike her contemporary, Catholic free women of color, Marie Aliquot or Henriette Delille, Marie could not found or run an order of nuns (the Holy Family Sisters) (Adams:360-367). Instead, she could and did become a priestess of Vodou.

Unlike the Church, in which priests often saw women as playing a role subservient to that of men, in Vodou men usually viewed women as possessors of mysterious power and strength. In fact the Congo-Niger language group of the contributors to the faith has no gender for nouns in their languages (Fandrich 1994:72), and the Yoruba, for example, still equate the unique power of women with that of men and consider it complementary in the religion, if not in all things. In Benin women actually dominate many devotional practices as they do in Vodou (Nevadomsky 1984:188; Metraux 1972:64-68).

Throughout Africa, even though leadership is often male, and women are not always full diviners, both men and women become priests who do jobs that are vital to the temple (Montenegro 1998:6). In some languages there is even no word for gender (Fandrich 1994). In Haitian Vodou, however, oungans (male priests) and mambos/queens (priestesses/head priestess) are completely equal and autonomous. This absolute power, due to their having been consecrated as vehicles to receive the will of Spirit, allows each complete freedom to affect religious practice, or as scholar Ina Fandrich put it, "remarkable individual power" (Fandrich 1994:78,79; Metraux 1972:158).

In the U.S., due to slavery, black men were often separated from their family while their women or offspring were often freed. Thus, women, separated from their men, had to take on leadership roles in the family and in religion. Moreover, in New Orleans, these women, many of them mambos, were born free and placed in common-law or marital-contract relationships with Creole and fpc men of power and wealth. Such women often gained political savvy and the opportunity to influence the society at large. Marie LaVeaux, for example, whose grandfather appears to have been Charles Trudeau, a famous New Orleans Creole involved in government, should have had the political connections to become an effective leader in New Orleans. (Fandrich 1994).

We know that the title given the chief initiate (oungan) in New Orleans Vodou was "king," and the woman who reigned with him or alone was "the queen." We know that Marie, at some point, ascended to that title with style, savvy, and the high level of community leadership it entailed, but how did she do it? Every detail is not clear, but here is one way of looking at the rest of her story and her ascension, step by step.

A Rocky Start

As a young woman, Marie seems to have had a rocky start even though she was born to a well-to-do merchant father. On Aug. 4, 1819, according to the Archdiocese records from St. Louis Cathedral, the priest, Pere Antoine (Fr. Antonio de Sedella) performed the marriage ceremony of Marie LaVeaux to Jacques (Santiago) Paris, a free quadroon (fmc), native of Santo Domingo (Haiti) (vol. 1-1777-1830: 59b/256). However, after less than one year of marriage, and (according to Liga Foley) soon after the death of Marie's mother, Marguerite Pomet D'Arcantel, Paris disappeared. As seen earlier, Liga said of this, "Marguerite, forced a carpenter to marry her because she couldn't account for her being pregnant."

After his departure, Marie called herself the widow Paris. Subsequently, according to Liga, she placed the illegitimate child she had carried while married to Paris (Delphine), in the care of an old servant named Chloe to be raised as white. (Delphine would later become Liga's mother.) Liga's account, true or not, tells us that, as a young person, Marie, though not financially imperiled, had her ups and downs. It also shows that Marie's mother must have died in the early 1820's before Marie met her life partner, Glapion, and recent findings concur (Long/Fandrich, email, 4/98).

Marie next learned a trade and, possibly with the help of her wealthy father, went into business, opening her own hair-dressing shop on Royal

St. Ultimately, by design, she became a hairdresser in the homes of rich Creole women. Along the way, according to an 1881 account attributed to Marie's youngest daughter, Philomene, she met the love of her life—Louis Christophe Duminy de Glapion. Glapion was a white Creole (born in New Orleans before American occupation and of European descent) and a former military man from an aristocratic New Orleans family. Such unions were not uncommon, but it was uncommon that Glapion resided with Marie. According to Philomene, they were together by 1821, although most reports say they married in '26 (Fandrich 1994).

After her marriage to Glapion, Marie lived simply in a small cottage that he purchased for her from Marie's mother's estate—the estate of Catherine Pomet Henri (Fandrich 1994). Many reports say that Marie got this cottage on St. Ann St. through Vodou, but Liga's tale explains that the story refers to the house on Toulouse St. that Marie was pressured to give to her daughter, Philomene, after she uncovered the secret of Marie's illegitimate child, Delphine. Said Liga,

> Let me tell you how Marie LaVeaux got this house she had to give Marie Philomene because of her pushings. She sure pulled the linchpin out of Marie's axel tree, and Marie flopped on her knees. See, Marie saved a rich man's son from the gallows by using a Vodou trick. I disremembers his name, but he was so grateful to end his torment, he gave her a decrepit mansion on Toulese [sic., Toulouse]....

Anyway, Philomene also reported that Marie LaVeaux was born in the little cottage on St. Ann St. Recent findings suggest that Marguerite d'Arcantel Henri, LaVeaux's mother, was related to Catherine Henri, the woman from whom Glapion made the purchase, so it is possible that Marie was born there (Long/Fandrich email 1998).

House of Love

Many rumors surround LaVeaux, but we do not know exactly when Marie became an initiate, much about the success of her career, or about her husband's source of income. However, some say that she saw great wealth from selling charms and giving readings to the rich. Certainly, money passed through her hands, but it must have passed right to her community and wards because she was not rich at the end of her life. There were many women of this name in the vicinity, and their stories sometimes became intermingled. Some say, that after being lost at sea, she swore off Vodou and lost her wealth (LRP 1930); some say that those rumors of wealth were caused by confusion with her wealthy half sister, also named Marie (de los Dolores) LaVeaux (ibid 1994), who died in France.

The naming customs in New Orleans are the source of much confusion. It seems that it was a French custom to name female, Catholic children Marie and Charles LaVeaux, Marie's father who divorced Marie's mother, followed that custom for his second marriage, naming his first daughter in that union Marie LaVeaux. This "Marie," who died young in France, did become quite wealthy and once lived near Marie, the Vodou queen (ibid 1994). She might also have resembled the Vodou queen as well. Accordingly, Marie LaVeaux herself named at least three of her girls Marie and simply called them by their middle or nicknames, leading to untold confusion amongst scholars: Marie Louise was called Caroline; Marie Philomene was called Philes or Philomene (later Mme.

Ligendre); and Marie Heloise Euchariste was called Euchariste, Epcaris, Marie Eloise, Eloise Euchariste, and some say, Clarisse! Euchariste succeeded her mother in Vodou, but died in 1862, causing her mother to return to her position as a leader in Vodou.

However, despite the confusion and whether or not she was wealthy, Marie LaVeaux was richly surrounded by love. She and her beloved Glapion had at least seven children, by my accounting, although her obituary says fifteen. Certainly the cottage grounds were said to have bustled with those whom the priestess dutifully sheltered (FWP folio 25).

Glapion, who had served with D'Aquino in the Haitian guard, lived with Marie, and so it comes as no surprise he was one of the white Creoles who (at least once) was listed as a free man of color. He lived in Maries world and (as did many men) he claimed their offspring (census, 1850). Only his death records clearly prove his race (Fandrich 1994). Moreover, the law might have prevented him from marrying a woman of color, but it did not prevent a wedding in Marie's tradition or an unofficial church ceremony (Weekly Picayune 1881; Long email 1998), one of which is assumed to have occurred.

For 29 years, St. Anne cottage would be their home. In the late 1830's, under American rule and the resultant chaos in the City, she and Glapion became quietly defiant. They purchased slaves only to set them free. In fact scholar Ina Fandrich believes that, around 1838, the Glapions were actually abolitionists (Fandrich email 1998), and it has been ascertained that the Underground Railroad had a New Orleans-Texas-Mexico route. Some do not accept this, but the record of their purchasing and then freeing slaves certainly does exist. If the Glapions were Underground Railroad operatives or sympathizers, this would have forged another connection between them and the operative called Mary Pleasant and attracted her to them. Nevertheless, during a time of chaos in the city, people from all walks of life, especially embattled Creoles, came for Marie's counsel and her Vodou charms. Granddaughter, Liga Foley recalled,

> I disremembers just exactly what year she [Marie] rebuilt her
> St. Anne St. cottage—before my time... She was possessed of so
> many visitors that came time to expand...

Corroborating, we find this 1930 Federal Writer's Project testimony,

> She has a house on St. Anne St., and people come from the ends
> of America to get help from her. Even Queen Victoria ask' her
> help and send her a cashmere shawl with money also (Federal
> Writer's Project).

By 1850, Mary Pleasant was among those who came to that cottage, but whoever came to 179 (later 152 and 1022) St. Ann St. found a house filled with the wealth of love and humanity. This is how Marie's power grew.

Chapter 9: Seizing Power

Enter Mam'zelle

But, what did LaVeaux do to become queen that finally garnered the interest of an activist like Mary Pleasant? When things in the City became unbearable, when the American regime began to bear down on Vodou, fpc's, and Creoles, she claimed her power. In Haiti and even Brazil, priestly positions are often gained by what is called family power—inheritance (Deren 1953), but in New Orleans, the most powerful priestesses vied to be queen. As mentioned, legend says that, in addition to study under the a well-known Senegalese priest named Dr. John, Marie apprenticed under Marie Saloppé, a queen who preceded her; however, it is also said that Marie eventually claimed the throne from Saloppé, physically vanquishing her in public (Fandrich 1994; FWP:folio 25; Tallant, ed. 1995).

The tale is probably embellished, but legend is replete with stories of Marie's boldness, and legend had a way of surrounding both LaVeaux and Pleasant. So we shall never know if it is true. Yet, the title was seized, and it is said that the crowd responded as they did for many years thereafter, calling her YeYe (beloved/esteemed mother), Mam'zelle Marie (Miss Marie). Here, in effect, is what they sang:

Eh Yeye, Mam'zelle Marie

O beloved Mother, Miss Marie

Ya, Yeye, li Konin tou, gris gris

Yes beloved Mother, who knows charms,

Li te kouri lekal, aver vieux kokodril

Who has studied those old crocodiles*

[*secrets of the messengers of Spirit]

Oh ouai, ye Mam'zelle Marie

Oh yes, venerable Miss Marie

Le konin bien li Grand Zombi

She knows him well --the Great Zombie (the spirit Damballah)

Legend or not, the truth of the song lay in the wisdom and ministering that this Vodou queen displayed. When the believers were destitute, the church (peopled by her cousins) prayed, but this queen helped them prosper. The offerings Mam'zelle helped them make often cleansed or relieved them of guilt and gave them leave to prosper. The money she received from the sale of charms and gris gris (protective pouches) often purchased their freedom. When there was illness, the priestess (an experienced nurse) brought herbs and healing prayers. When there was injustice, she conjured revenge, leading the ancient rituals and dances. She was bold enough once to storm the courts to preserve her power from a competing Vodou priestess, and when the power of love failed for a devotee, the priestess sometimes stirred it with a potion.

In keeping with her vision, Marie formalized worship of Li Grand Zombi (Bodin 1990:22) and prescribed prayer to the saints—which ever (saint, ancestor, or loa) suited the purpose at hand. Marie, the bride and "horse" (one often possessed) of Damballah, could channel him for her people. And when Lwa came down and "rode her," she became a "direct connection." As queen, Marie certainly seemed to be, as Liga said, "the mouthpiece of God" (Foley 1930).

The LaVeaux Model

A Closer Look

Such is a poetic way of looking at the feats of Marie LaVeaux, but some of her accomplishments deserve closer examination. In 1994, Luisah Teish, Ph.D., whose work merges three African-based traditions (African, Cuban, and New Orleanean) responded to a pattern of activity between the work of Marie LaVeaux and Mary Pleasant, which I described to her by saying, "Oh, the LaVeaux Model." In so doing, she coined a useful phrase. For in comparing Pleasant's work in San Francisco with that of LaVeaux, I noticed parallels—the same elements being used in the same sequence to the same effect, and so I adopted Teish's phrase to describe LaVeaux's key social and political activities.

According to Dr. Teish (Teish 1985) and most scholars, Marie, a talented healer, used certain saints as part of her healing/vodou prescriptions. She also became one of the first to develop the widespread sale of charms and gris-gris amongst the wealthy, the first to popularize her faith at large and to be able to protect it socially and politically. Thus she was the first known to use Vodou in leveraging secrets to force the City's powerful to aid the powerless—the condemned, the poor, her followers, and others who sought her help. Each element of LaVeaux's model has been documented through testimonies, many of which can be found in Folio 25 of the Louisiana portion of the Federal Writer's Project (FWP) of the 1930's.

Gaining Leverage

It is often alleged that Marie possessed secrets that she leveraged for favors amongst "the powers that be" in New Orleans, but how did she do that? One technique for this, which Pleasant later employed in the West, was the use of devotees who worked for wealthy Creoles as domestic spies. They simply passed the secrets of their employers to Marie at special gatherings in her back yard, thereby giving Marie leverage with them to ask favors for some needy person. Liga provided a measure of confirmation of this when she said,

> *Nights—never in moonlight—when Marie held Vodou gatherings in the back yard, me and her youngest sometimes watched. Fact is, these were held for the purpose of picking up gossip from the close help [live-in servants] of prominent New Orleans houses. Mostly women and a few men in fancy breeches. -Mostly couldn't stop 'em from talking no how, and they' owners hadn't a notion [where] those from lower down [downstairs help] was spendin' they time when [they not] tending to they chores.*

A second element of her leveraging technique was matchmaking. Marie matched wealthy men with women of lower station under the contracting process called Le Placage at a meeting place that she called "La Maison Blanche." There she could forge placage arrangements and liasons that might later create allies within wealthy families for her causes. Some say this La Maison Blanche was run by her daughter; others attribute it to this Marie. Certainly, since Mary Pleasant copied this practice and once created a similar place called Geneva Cottage, we have reason to believe that the first Marie LaVeaux started this practice. After being "matched" by Marie, women held an allegiance to her and are said to have supported her causes. Of her matchmaking events at the special place, one observer recalled,

> *At the real hoodoo dances she had people coming from all over the world. It was true there was lots of white men and yellow gals at that house. Marie LaVeaux did that for money... The only music they used was a drum made out of a barrel with a piece of skin stretched over it, and she hired a black to beat that with his hands* (FWP: Folio 25).

A third element of LaVeaux's model, in addition to pressuring the affluent and powerful using their secrets, was aiding the powerful all over the world (for a price), to garner not only their help, but also, their respect and gratitude. Pleasant later did the same. For example, LaVeaux helped many Americans, who had taken over New Orleans in 1803 and persecuted her people, the Creoles. Using her influence amongst such City officials (along with her Vodou "work") LaVeaux is said to have secured release from the threat of imprisonment for the relatives of wealthy Creoles and others. For twenty-one years she also ministered to the condemned—those who could not gain release (Weekly Picayune; Louisiana Press Democrat 6/17/1881).

Marie LaVeaux then used this gratitude at the proper moments to help others. In return for using her priestly skills to become powerful amongst the powerful of the City, she gained protection for her religion, which was under attack. One man remembers how, during the height of the persecution of Vodou, when well-known Vodou practitioners, such as Betsy Toledano, were being arrested for holding ceremony, Marie held ceremonies protected by police and held the power to order the police out of a gathering (Fandrich 1994),

> *When the police come messin' around she would holler at em'.*
> *Shut the goddam door! There wasn't no door when they was out*
> *there in the open, but that meant for them to go away because*
> *they wasn't wanted. And they used to get out* (Tallant, Voodoo
> in New Orleans: 56, 57 per FWP: folio 25).

Congo Square

A fourth element of her model was raising the morale and safety of her people through pubic displays of her power in the mainstream society. Marie seems to have maintained her traditional duties as a priest and healer. As a nurse, according to one obituary, she was actually drafted by the people of the city to serve in two of New Orleans' great plagues (Weekly Picayune, 6/18/81). Marie also "healed" her followers through popularizing Vodou in staged public ceremonies at Lake Ponchartrain and through what have been called "decoy dances" in Congo Square (also called Louis Armstrong Sq.)—cultural dances, such as the Calinda, which white onlookers mistook for real Vodou ceremonials. In her book on worldwide seasonal celebration, (Teish 1997:143), Luisah Teish calls Congo Square "the Apollo of New Orleans." Certainly it was the showplace for African culture in New Orleans. Jazz emerged from events there, but the healing that Marie secured for her people there by sustaining the "decoy" dances through times of oppression was perhaps her greatest protective service.

Dance anthropologists, historians, and priests, such as the great dancer-anthropologist Katherine Dunham, have long reported that, in African culture, dance is both a means of worship, of ego development, of "knowing," and of psychological release (Osumare 1998; Thompson, 1978: Drewal 1984). That means that the dances themselves in Congo Square were more than just emotionalism. At a time when Vodou was feared and outlawed, its practitioners persecuted, these dances were important sources of pride. To see officials, whom Marie had invited, actually attend them surely served as a tonic to their spirits. Said one witness,

> *I tell you this. She was a great person. I don't care what nobody says. Sometimes policemens tried to keep Marie LaVeaux out, but she jest hypnotized 'em and walked in ... Well when she got in the middle of the square, she took her snake out of the box and danced wit it. When she got through dancin', all the other folks dance, not before. I tell you, she could make anybody do anything* (Tallant, Voodoo in New Orleans: 56, 57 per FWP: Folio 25).

Mam'zelle raised heads and hearts through the defiance of public bans and her display of power over tyranny in Congo Square. Lesser members might have fled when the police threatened, but Marie LaVeaux stood and triumphed or provided devotees with an alternative site. In so doing, she became "really cool"—the stuff of legends. The witness continued,

She could have a policeman fired with one snap of her fingers, and she could get one promoted with two snaps. Sometimes she just walked out into a big policeman's office and said [something like] "Do it! I is Marie LaVeaux and I wants it done." And he knew bettr'n not to do. If he didn't, something awful bad was sure gonna happen to him. That's the truth....You may not believe it, but that woman was the real boss of New Orleans! (Tallant 1946: 86-87; FWP: folio 25)

It was to this model of power that Mary Pleasant was drawn.

The Marie LaVeaux Model

	Actions of LaVeaux in New Orleans	Actions of Mary Pleasant in San Francisco
1	Buying and manumitting slaves	Rescuing slaves and getting writs to keep them in CA
2	Serving the rich lovingly through assistance and spiritual work, thereby engendering gratitude and assistance for her causes.	Serving the rich lovingly through assistance and spiritual work, thereby engendering gratitude and assistance for her causes.
3	Using domestic spies to gain secrets and matchmaking to create internal family pressure in favor of her causes.	Using domestic spies to gain secrets and matchmaking to create internal family pressure in favor of her causes.
4	Displaying her power in court battles and other public venues to raise the morale and help her people.	Displaying her power in court battles and other public venues to raise the morale and help her people.

Chapter 10: Moving West

The Arrival

According to her 1880's scribe, Charlotte Downs, Mary Pleasant had been told of her destiny as a priestess of Vodou by her mother, said to have been a Haitian Vodou queen and the daughter of a queen. Mary would therefore have known that, through family power, she was destined to help her people. "If they rise, I rise" says one version of an old proverb, enjoining daily dedication to community. Well known New Orleans mambo and Yoruba priestess Ava K. Jones said of this, "Vodou is my religion and my life," Oungan Elmer Glover concurred (Bibbs interviews 1996). Thus, no matter how far away from the practice of her faith Mary Pleasant went, she could not have left her destiny and Lwa far behind.

She would have seen them at the Ursaline Convent in New Orleans, where as a child she was taken immediately after being removed from slavery (MEP/Davis 1901). She might have recognized her spirit forces hidden in the faint smiles of the stoic saints there. No doubt, finding the release and praise of her religion in the catechism, so unlike the possessions and praises of Vodou ceremony, might have been difficult. Still, Mary's afro-centric vantage point would have allowed her to embrace the more somber Catholic approach and, later, the silent Quaker meeting, to accept others and to find her Lwa wherever she went. Ultimately her destiny led her to Marie LaVeaux.

The Departure

Definitely, her timing was good. Liga, the LaVeaux look-alike whom Marie had chosen to succeed her, was unwilling and would soon actually run away rather than serve. Liga completed the story of her escape (excerpted earlier), which details her refusal to accept Marie's power. Although this may resemble some other recorded accounts of ceremony, one must remember that Liga did not read them. Did Helen Holdredge, who recorded the interview, add anything? We shall never know—

> Her followers demanded, but I had a horror of snakes—I sure did. I had a niggling suspicion I would be required to hold a snake over my head if I followed in her footsteps, and I decided, although I didn't know where I'd be going, I'd get out of there! But Marie decided I'd see one of her Vodou rituals, and I was then at sixteen or seventeen. Just before that night, I tried to ship out somewhere—anywhere—but she fetched me up proper, and I found myself on the shore of Lake Ponchartrain as an observer, although I was convinced I'd hate it. And I was higher than a cat's back with apprehension....
>
> Sure enough Marie interpreted messages relayed to her through the Great Serpent [Damballah] who lived at the foot of God. She was the sanctuary of power. A bonfire blazed in a nearby clearing. There were nine lighted candles on the ground and bottles of what was probably tafia [rum brew] between the candles, and the box with the snake inside. Marie's hair—long, black, and

curly like my own—was spread out over her shoulders. She was dressed in blue [one of the colors of good works and Damballah's brides], her large breasts exposed at the neckline. For a full hour the Negroes adored the snake, petitioning the Great Serpent to speak to them and also [they] made promises. Marie then danced on the box with the snake, imitating his motions. Her followers also danced; clapped their hands and pounded the ground with their feet. This was all done to the beating of a drum. The dancers drank the cheap rum from the bottles and, tearing off their clothes, climaxed the ceremony by rushing off to the woods in pairs. [When]The pat time was over, I fled out to the road...(HH/Foley 1930)

Mary Pleasant had no such feelings or fears, and so under LaVeaux's guidance, she would have learned to become an oracle for Damballah, learned to comfort, control, and guide followers, learned how to "encourage" non-believers to serve her causes, and to forge equality with enterprise. Her qualification to be shown these secrets supports the idea that Pleasant had a background in Vodou, something that her second husband once recounted to a friend. Mary embraced the "LaVeaux" model to prepare for the West. However, the trip came all too soon.

The Flying Cloud ship Mt. Pleasant once said JJ took to San Francisco in 1851

Escape to the West

Soon after their arrival in New Orleans, and some say shortly after their legal marriage enroute to New Orleans aboard Capt. Gardner's ship, Mary's new husband, JJ, decided to sail west to scout a new, safer life for them both. The truth was that JJ, born free, could not share Mary's deep passion for causes although he often worked in her abolition activities. Certainly JJ was humane, but Mary suggested in her final memoir that his strongest passions lay with her wealth, flashy clothes, life as a seafaring chef, good liquor, and Mary—in that order (Davis/MEP 1901). So JJ headed West, and Mary stayed behind to study (Downs 1930).

LaVeaux scholar Ina Fandrich and researcher Mary Millan believe that LaVeaux and Glapion might even have been a Southern terminus for underground railroad activities in the area, (Fandrich 1998; Millan email 1998). Certainly, according to the Downs' account of Pleasant's memoir, Marie helped fugitive-rescuer Mary get a job as a cook at a plantation nearby. Soon Mary, with the help of an abolitionist cohort, began (as she had in the North) disguising herself again as the elusive "Negro" jockey—that is, a black jockey who was transported for racing from plantation to plantation. Legend says, once there, she would alert slaves of impending escapes. Of course, once again, as the elusive jockey, who seemed to appear and disappear, Mary became much hunted by slavers and local plantation holders, and of course, once again she was forced to flee.

The Fugitive Slave Law of 1850 intensified the capture of escaped slaves and their rescuers. To do so, it authorized commissioners to decide the fate of escapees, in lieu of the local courts, deputized unwilling bystanders, and levied stiff penalties for aiding or rescuing escapees. It also paid slave catchers and commissioners double to return, rather than release any captives. Pressures soon increased on Mary Pleasant and interrupted her study with Mam'zelle LaVeaux. Fortunately this occurred in 1851 just after JJ had sent for her to come to San Francisco (MEP/Davis 1902). Downs told the story of the escape as Pleasant had told it to her in the early 1880's,

> *In order to hide her when the chase got too close, Marie LaVeaux got employment for Mammy [a nickname given Pleasant] as a plantation cook.... There she busied herself trying out New Orleans dishes.... The planter there bragged about her cooking to some friends. Mammy knew this might lead to trouble when someone among them might*

guess she was the mysterious jockey who had seemingly disappeared. So, she decided to make an escape.

Putting on her shawl as though she was going out to the privy, she fled to Marie's house but not hurriedly. She walked right down the road. In case someone would stop her, she carried a folded white paper in her hand, which she had herself written—servants were not supposed to read or write. The note was vaguely signed "M." Sure enough, two men on horseback stopped her. One of them said to her, "What's going on here!" The other man asked her if it [the note] was not a billet-doux [love note] to which she made a firm denial and said the message was very private. Then the first man said that it really didn't concern him, and she'd better hurry because the plantation gates would be locked for the night where she was going. When she appeared at Marie LaVeaux's, the Vodou queen said something like, "You plannin' on goin' somewhere, honey!" She got passage for Mammy as "Mme. Christophe" on a ship going to California. This was in the autobiography that Mrs. Pleasant dictated to me (HH/Downs 1930).

Thus, presumably, as an initiate of the Great Zombie (Damballah), armed with her heritage of power through Mam'zelle LaVeaux, Mary sailed to California, ultimately to become its Mother of Civil Rights.

CONGO SQUARE

(This poetic homage to Marie LaVeaux recounts both her legend and actual acheivements)

Saunter down old Rampart Street

Stop, inhale the air

Tip your hat to good Saint Anne

Then enter Congo Square.

Raise your left foot lightly;

Three times lay it down,

Bend your knees so slightly now

To kiss the hallowed ground.

Look upon your kindred, chil',

The rocks, the trees, the birds;

Speak to them all silently,

The river's voice is heard.

There the spirits whisper

Here the dead are fair.

Now the Great Zombie appears

In the circle in Congo Square.

Below the green grass trembles,

Above, the full moon sings.

Spirit moves both in and out,

Between and through all things.

Heritage of Power

A cheese-box drum is played now,
With the jaw-bone of an ass.
Women don their finest whites,
Some slaves, some upper class.

Brick dust marks the circle
Red against black earth;
White clay marks the brow bone
Of the one marked for rebirth.

There's taffia and water,
And feathers stained with blood.
River spirits dance and drink
For heat, drought, and the flood.

All the men are agile
All the women fair,
All the spirits leap and run
'Round the circle in Congo Square.

Piled high, wood is burning,
black cauldron filled with oil.
The faithful step forth bravely,
While the charlatans recoil.
Now is the magic moment
The test of truth is here.

Only the devoted plunge their hands
In the pot of oil without fear.

Those who pass have honor.
Those who fail must go.
Only true believers pass
The test of Hunzi Canzo.

The spirits hover low now,
The people shout and dance,
The serpent wraps himself around
The queen in her proud prance.
She showers all with blessings
"La Reine de Jardiniere"
Mam'zelle LaVeaux frees all the slaves
In the circle in Congo Square.

All the trees are swaying
As the warm gulf breezes blow,
And spores are gently landing
Where Spanish moss will grow.

All the men are howling
As all the women flirt.
Toil and tears with blood and rum
Sink down into the dirt.

Then all the joy is fractured
When cannon's boom is heard.
And so, the dance must end now
As the Law has sent the word.
And all the people exit
And scatter everywhere,
Taking the magic with them,
Leaving shadows in Congo Square.

But from the Square they venture
To the house on old St. Anne;
Or, behind the doors of "La Maison Blanche,"
Mam'zelle unfolds her plan.

Inside she shelters runaways,
Takes poor girls off the street.
She purifies and teaches them,
In a manner most discreet.

The queen will soon adorn them
And start the Quadroon Ball.
She'll mate them there through Le Placage
Behind her cottage walls.

Their children will be born there,
The old and sick will heal.
Her gumbo, sent to those condemned,
gives death a peaceful meal.

And when the slaves revolted
Against their wretched lot,
Mam'zelle Marie is found to be
The mistress of the plot.
She listens to the stories
The upper crust has told
Then turns the tales against them
In a manner brave and bold.

She could kill or cure with plants,
With thought or with a hand.
She knew the herbs of Africa,
Of Haiti, and this land.
Men of high class loved her
Some came from far away.
Rumor says she received a shawl
From the emperor of China one day.

We know of Square and cottage
Yet mysteries remain
Deep in the waters of Bayou St. John
And the waters of Pontchartrain.
For there they walked through fire,
Danced on water and through the air,
Performing the ancient African rites
Never seen in Congo Square.

Author Luisah Teish in the role of Marie LaVeaux
in On My Journey, a musical chautauqua by Susheel Bibbs, 1994

Chapter 11: Early Days in San Francisco

Movin' West

Mary sailed to San Francisco on a steamer around the Horn, but there is controversy over her departure—The Downs account says New Orleans; another says New York. Mary herself named two different ships and never a point of departure! Fortunately, however, we can document her entry into California via her final ship. Thus, despite her claim to have arrived in '49, Mary Ellen Pleasant arrived in San Francisco on the Steamer Oregon, April 7, 1852, listed as "Mme. Christophe," her husband's true surname (SF Ships Passage records, vol. 3). A charming young merchant/broker named Thomas Bell boarded the Oregon in Acapulco. This Scotsman would eventually become the beloved partner with whom Mary would amass her fortune!

A Rough 'n Ready Place

Fleas, Glass, and Mud

1850's San Francisco had 40-50,000 people (few women) and anywhere from 400 to 700 drinking houses and saloons, depending on who was counting. Over 1 million gallons of liquor per year flowed into the locals there, resulting in five murders every six days (Lockwood 1978). So wet were the winters that a new theatre once sank down inches in the mud; horses died there, causing an infestation of fleas. Locals also threw down their all-too-plentiful liquor bottles to form paths so that they would not sink as well. Yet, although this place of new beginnings was not the safe haven Mary had sought, she was up to the challenge.

Mary waited several months before working, but finally chose as her employers the boarding club of commission merchants Case and Heiser because it housed the City's richest men. She had arrived in rough 'n ready San Francisco, unfortunately, just after California's own version of the Fugitive Slave Law, one of the stiffest in the country, had been enacted (followed her) there. So, having no proof of her freedom, she was forced into covert activity (spying) once again.

Muddy Feet on Velvet

Until 1852 most gold-rush inmates (merchants, miners, investors, etc.) were enormously wealthy and without wives. San Francisco might have been a desolate, muddy, flea-infested place, but its wealthy still wanted their muddy feet nursed on velvet cushions, so they often established very opulent housing collectives where they could sleep, eat lavish meals, do business, drink, and play cards. These they called boarding houses (Lockwood ibid), and to avoid being wrested into slavery Mary managed several, passing as Mrs. Ellen Smith, a white steward (supervising cook and housekeeper).

Using the Model

Mrs. Ellen Smith

Many historians and even a doctoral dissertation (Hudson, 1996) seem to have misunderstood Mary's early employment there and in boarding establishments of the day. Seeming to forget that she arrived as a wealthy woman and unaware of the LaVeaux model, they have characterized her merely as a crafty servant. Missing the "Ellen Smith" pseudonym, some have either failed to credit her with her early social accomplishments or to see that she placed herself in disguise to avoid false arrest under the California Fugitive Slave Law and to implement the Marie LaVeaux model, which called for domestic spying on and match making for the powerful in order to serve the powerless. In addition to spying on her wealthy boarders to leverage secrets for her people, Mary also gained investment tips from them and became their caretaker, often preparing extra food and wines for club members who were volunteer firefighters or vigilantes (Downs 1930).

The Franchise League

In 1850's San Francisco, as Pleasant put leveraging to work, she also aided slaves brought into the City. Miners in California did not want slaves to be brought into the state to work the mines to unfair advantage; however, judges who sympathized with the South simply looked the other way as slaves were brought in. Many free states, including California, enacted restrictions called "black laws" to discourage slavers and people of color from settling there. Under these laws, blacks could be set free if they were put to work or free blacks paid some miscellaneous taxes and could not serve in the militia or testify in court. They were thus unprotected from all-too-prevalent theft, claim jumping, and assault. They were disenfranchised.

In San Francisco a man named Miflin Gibbs, who was later to become the first black ambassador to Madagascar, gathered abolitionist cohorts, white and black, from New Bedford and other places to form an activist group called the Franchise League. Its primary purpose was to use the law to oppose the black laws and to enfranchise the so-called "colored" populous of California. To this end they circulated petitions for the right to testify in court (Right of Testimony) and sponsored several "Colored Conventions" (1855, 56, 57, and 65) to determine the needs and best direction for the "colored" community. They also forged The Mirror of the Times, the first "colored" newspaper in California, as a voice for the people, and they secured lawyers and writs for slaves who were to be taken from California back into slavery. Mary Pleasant covertly supported this group in the 50's and would later overtly lead it (HH/WillmoreJr: 24, 26).

In the 1850's, the repeal of the black laws and the support of ex-slaves in California became her field. As Ellen Smith, she "encouraged" the wealthy to give to "her favorite causes" (Thurman 1996), and as Mrs. Pleasants, she secretly rode to rescue ex-slaves in the fields, openly appearing on the docks with writs to stop their extradition. After conducting interviews with elders who remembered Pleasant or held family remembrances, historian Sue B. Thurman, who first called her "Mother of Civil Rights in California," once wrote,

> *Negroes who remember her will tell you about how many times she went out into the rural part of the country to rescue slaves who were being held illegally by masters recently come to California... will mention the vigorous role she played during the Negro's fight for the Right of Testimony...[and] say they saw little of her until some oppressed member of her group got into difficulties. Then she would put all her privilege and prestige at his disposal* (Thurman 1949).

As Mrs. Thurman explained to me in a 1996 interview, Mary (first known to California blacks as Mrs. Pleasants) helped the Franchise

League fight the black-laws and called upon her wealthy "friends" to support their efforts financially. She personally helped many blacks establish their own businesses and smuggled escaped slaves into the State, employing them in her many enterprises. In effect, she became a one-woman community-development system.

Capitalist by Trade

Continuing the LaVeaux model, which required that Pleasant create supporters within wealthy families, Pleasant removed girls who displayed promise from the City's seedy Dupont St. bordellos, educated them, and made Placage-like matches for them with City luminaries. As did LaVeaux, she became a matchmaker as a niche (special audience) enterprise.

Although she twice invested in bordellos to gain leverage for help from the men who participated, she was never "a madam," as would later be alleged by her enemies. Rather, for that job Pleasant hired the famous madam Victoria Perrit (HH25/WWJr). Mary was neither prude nor saint—As a mambo, she was creative and did what worked to help her people. She was also a survivor and a woman of the old West. However, bordellos were not regarded then as they are today. Men outnumbered women six to one in 1850's San Francisco, and their girl friends and wives were far away, so their dates, dances, dinners, and holiday celebrations revolved around bordellos unless they wanted to dance alone or with each other. Bordello Balls and weekend promenades with the ladies who worked there were common. The ladder of success for many a San Francisco socialite began there. So, Mary was an entrepreneur, and she saw a niche that she hoped she could leverage to help her people. She upgraded her bordellos to make them appealing to rich Southerners. However, the business did not prove profitable for her, even if it did produce some wives who might later become her allies. She later sold her bordellos or converted them to legitimate boarding houses.

Later, to instate the LaVeaux Placage/leveraging model of using matchmaking to gain internal allies in rich families, Mary Pleasant created an exclusive rendezvous haunt outside of the City, which she called Geneva Cottage (Gould 1987). Even though Mary thought that Geneva Cottage (a niche enterprise) would be welcomed by her Southern boarding-house clients, its lavish $500 per night formal dinners and fetes did not prove substantially appealing to them. She held the secrets of the liaisons, problems, and marriages forged there. However, Pleasant's bordellos and Geneva Cottage (unlike La Maison Blanche) were not successful, and she closed them. San Francisco was not New Orleans (Holdredge 1953).

Pleasant invested in everything and had successes that brought wealth and jobs for her people. She invested profitably in boarding houses, railroads, a library, and a saloon. She loved land and held enormous amounts of it. She held lateral (support) enterprises for her boarding house businesses—tenant farms, dairy farms, a saloon, a livery stable, laundries. In fact, she once listed herself as "Mary Pleasant, capitalist."

Hoodoo House

During the 1860's Liga Foley, LaVeaux's "runaway" granddaughter, served as the live-in steward (head housekeeper) for what became one of many homes for which Pleasant served as steward-at-large—a sort of consulting, party-planning position. Liga, as resident steward in Sen. Latham's house, worked with Pleasant periodically and was able to clarify her genuine charity and her duties in these homes. Her employment in those homes for years has confused scholars, so this is important. Was she a cook and servant or something else? Liga clarified—

[She was a] *"female steward," but it was actually a held stewardship before Fred gave up entertaining. Of course, "it didn't hold good" that she actually kept house for Mr. Latham.*

In her patois, Liga meant that Pleasant, a steward on retainer who supervised entertainment for several wealthy householders, was not a regular housekeeper. Among her retainers were Fred Woodworth, the City's richest man, and Liga's boss Southerner/ex-Senator Milton Latham. Much as an exclusive decorator might do today, Pleasant served various households regularly in this way. Later when trying to play up her simplicity and service during court battles, she would confuse matters by talking of cooking and cleaning, but she most often supervised those duties, and in the case of Liga's house, she did not perform them at all. Liga supervised Latham's house, and Pleasant planned events. Liga called the house Hoodoo (the hexed) House because a string of its owners met with misfortune and death while living there. Liga, as head housekeeper remained, as the house maintained a string of wealthy unfortunates.

Liga had secretly spied on Pleasant's doings in New Orleans with Mam'zelle, but was never really seen by Pleasant there. Still, she feared being recognized by Pleasant for her uncanny resemblance to LaVeaux, and when she was forced to see Mrs. "Smith" almost daily for a time because of her work at the house, she reports being terrified (HH/Foley 1930). Liga described her feelings and one "teasing" encounter with Pleasant this way—

> *Mrs. Pleasant had a knowledge of something I had collided with... She specified I was to visit her and that wasn't at all explainable. When I arrived at her boarding house, we settled down on a sofa. She almost stopped my mind when she said she 'membered who I remind her of—Marie LaVeaux...I was filled with wonderment over this I swear that thinking on it scared me. Mrs. Pleasant began the conversation "most kindly" by saying I reminded her of Marie LaVeaux, who she had known in New Orleans. It was soon obvious that the woman didn't think I had any connections [or so Liga thought] because she launched into the story of Marie's curse on her granddaughter at a voodoo ceremony. The girl had run away with a white planter and when she tried to stop him he killed her and threw her body to the alligators in the bayou. This was confirmed by a bloody piece of the dress the girl had worn found in a thorny bush... I had many thoughts returning and almost fell over the styleblock when I got into Mrs. Latham's carriage. (ibid 1930)*

Genuine Reciprocation

Despite fear of her, Liga praised Pleasant's charity and ambition. Being typical of the vision of a great mambo, her generous nature and personal charity impressed Liga. In her interviews, Liga says that Mary voluntarily nursed "Hoodoo House" owner Fred Woodworth until his death of throat cancer in 1865 and was distraught after his death. Fred, his brother Selim, and Selim's wife Lisette had been Pleasant's supporters since her early days as a steward at The Case-Heiser commission merchant's boarding house and would remain long-term friends.

Liga clarified Pleasant's role as a steward-friend to her employers, when she told the story of Senator Latham's wife: In 1867, Mrs. Latham was tormented to the point of insanity by something mysterious. Disturbed, Latham brought Pleasant in to counsel. Said Liga in her interviews with author Helen Holdredge,

> *Her presence was like a breath of mountain air to Mrs. Latham. It was not long before Mrs. Pleasant uncovered what was Sophie Latham's trouble. In crossing the plains, she had killed many animals for food. Now, when she tried to sleep, they all surrounded her, with pleading eyes not to kill them.*

Pleasant counseled the woman patiently back to mental health— this, despite concern for the Senator's reputed anti-black sympathies. Nevada controller and editor Sam P. Davis, Pleasant's final biographer, called her a genuine lover of human beings and cited many examples of her charity in the 1904 obituary that he wrote for Pleasant. Here is one excerpt—

> *It is told on the best of authority that when her old employer, Capt. Johns [of the Case Heiser house] died in straitened circumstances, she [Mary] advanced the money to send the family East and for years assisted at least in their support* (Davis: SF Chronicle 1904).

Like Martin Luther King of our times, Pleasant's courage and "heart" were unparalleled. As a pupil of Marie LaVeaux and as initiate, Mary was enjoined to love humans apart from differences, and it seems to have come naturally. Regardless of her causes, she would "walk the extra mile" for a person in need, regardless of race or class. In fact, she once said jokingly that it was easy to give charity to the rich because they would never repay it. This did not prove true. Without losing sight of the needs and trials of her people, she would remain a friend until the end, and years after her time at Case-Heiser and at Hoodoo House, when these merchants became City luminaries, Pleasant's fortune and power to effect change through them grew. Through these men, she was able to effect another part of the LaVeaux model —the exchange of gratitude for favors. Obviously, her power was not, as the tabloids often reported, due simply to her storehouse of secrets on their pasts, but rather, as with LaVeaux, to genuine reciprocation.

Black City Hall

Legend says that in 1869 Mary became San Francisco's first (and perhaps only) Vodou queen. There is no proof, but certainly, in completion of LaVeaux's model, this would have been a natural step. As queen, she held secrets gained through domestic informants that she traded for favors (Downs1930; HH/WW Jr), and as a friend to the rich, she received reciprocation for her people. For example, she opened the first home catering jobs for "colored" people at Senator Latham's lavish parties, and Latham, a Southern sympathizer who was so indebted to Pleasant, could not object. Of this, his housekeeper, Liga Foley said,

Mrs. Pleasant worked plenty to get Negroes in on these, and they floated to the surface—being satisfactory. I mean Latham didn't like it much, but he needed her knowledge about such affairs...

The Latham parties set a trend and opened the doors to jobs in other homes for the first time. Later Mary would pressure and get jobs for "colored" citizens in hotels and on steamers, and in the 1870's, on the railroad. According to historian B. Gordon Wheeler, Pleasant's responses to the appeals of her people and the amazing changes in opportunity for them that resulted soon earned her the nickname "The Black City Hall." Colored citizens did not know how, but when Pleasant acted in their behalf, things happened!

Depiction by California historian Beach Alexander of a Milton Latham fete, courtesy of the artist.

Chapter 12. A Friend of John Brown

What Pleasant Said

Pleasant fought oppression as did LaVeaux, but her work took on national significance in 1858 and '59, when she aided abolitionist John Brown with his raid on the federal arsenal at Harper's Ferry, then in Virginia. Pleasant kept her involvement with Brown a secret, but a few years before her death, she revealed this chapter of her life to her final biographer, Nevada Controller and editor Sam P. Davis. At that time she asserted a desire to have "A Friend of John Brown" inscribed on her tombstone.

Pleasant asserted to Davis that she had 1) given Brown $30-40,000 of her own money during a meeting with him and his son in Canada in support of his planned raid on the Federal arsenal at Harpers Ferry, VA, 2) purchased land in Chatham Canada West (Ontario) for a slave refuge as part of Brown's plan, and 3) returned East in 1859, once again posing as a jockey, to alert slaves in southern Virginia of Brown's plan and to encourage them to join him.

Pleasant provided Davis with names, places, and a letter with directions to enable him to confirm her story (Pleasant Letter 1902, 6-pg Letter). This he did, and he published his findings in an article entitled How A Colored Woman Aided John Brown in Maine's Comfort Magazine in1903. The article was quoted and reprinted as late as 1940, and although Davis's account was compelling, some historians still dismissed him and his article, and many who never saw it continued to consider the story one of the many legends of Pleasant's colorful life. (Davis 1903. Conrich 1940. Warr 1975:4. Moss 2007).

How A Colored Woman Aided John Brown

A Piece of Unwritten History Disclosing the Identity of the Mysterious Backer of the Hero of Harper's Ferry.

BY SAM P. DAVIS.

Sam Davis' article based on unpublished memoirs
in Maine's Comfort Magazine, 1903

Brown's Plan

John Brown was not mad or deranged as some have claimed. Research shows that he and his plan have been much misunderstood. Since many have doubted Pleasant's involvement with Brown's plan, it is important to detail it and to document that involvement. So what was this plan? Brown sought to siphon off slaves from Virginia plantations, raising Vanguard slave militias and a free zone in the Virginia hills, and ferreting some slaves to refuge land in Canada West (now Ontario), where Mary Pleasant and others had purchased slave refuge land (Libby 2003, Geffert, 2002, H/GR: deed 1858; MEP/Davis letters undated, 1903; Delaca fragment, undated). By withdrawing valuable slaves in this way, Brown hoped to upset the economic balance of the South, ultimately pressuring them into ending slavery. In 1894, Brown's friend, writer James Hamilton, put it this way,

He had for many years been studying the guerilla system of warfare adopted in the mountainous portions of Spain and

the Caucasus, and in a ruder manner, by the Maroons of Jamaica[sic].… He thought he could with a small body of picked men inaugurate and maintain a negro insurrection [sic] in the mountains of Virginia—more successful than the Roman Spartacus, and cause so much annoyance to the United States government, and dread in the minds of slaveholders that they would ultimately be glad to "let the oppressed go free" (Hamilton 1894: 11).

Historian Hannah Geffert corroborates that Brown did plan to ferret many slaves from the insurrection in Virginia along Harriet Tubman's Appalachian escape route, called The Great Black Way, to Canada West (the Chatham area), thereby damaging slavery by creating a "bleeding" of slaves (Geffert 2002: 594).

Moreover, by arming his militias with the 90-100,000 repeating rifles housed at the Harper's Ferry arsenal, Brown expert Jean Libby asserts that Brown expected to magnify their force. He selected Harper's Ferry because it was not guarded by Federal troops, said Brown scholar Louis DeCaro—all in all a feasible plan. He proceeded with only 21 men, white and black, who joined him from Chatham, Ontario, and other places. He failed because he changed his time of action and hesitated at critical junctures during the raid—sometimes in an effort to save lives (Libby, DeCaro 2003).

Easy Confirmations

Pleasant first became involved with Brown's plan when she learned, through a letter from her former sister in law, Mrs. Dunn of

Philadelphia and Ohio, that Dunn's husband had been re-enslaved under the Fugitive Slave Act of 1850. At the same time, 1858, economic depression was decreasing the population of San Francisco drastically, and unrest had surfaced in the very active "colored" community over unfairness in the courts and pressure from the California legislature to restrict their rights. The result had been the disheartening exodus of Miflin Gibbs and many other leaders of San Francisco's "colored"-rights movements to Fraser Valley (Victoria, Canada). That's when Mary decided that she and JJ would go back East to Ontario, not to relocate permanently, but to help Mr. Dunn and to help John Brown end slavery by any means necessary!

Said Pleasant,

> I was informed that there was a man, John Brown, who had a plan to free all the slaves with help…I met John Brown. I found him stopping with one son at a boarding house on King St. kept by a man named Barbour…I went to Nantucket for the money, it being on deposit there… after which I met him in Philadelphia (Memoir, 1901; Letter dictated to Mrs. S.)

Pleasant says further that she went to Chatham to purchase land for a slave refuge for those that Brown would rescue. After rescuing Mr. Dunn, she made him caretaker of this land. While in Chatham, she participated wtih the local slave advocacy group, The Vigilance Committee.

There is proof of Pleasant's assertions. The deed to Mary and John Pleasant's property in Chatham, Canada West (Ontario) has now been found. In addition, as shown below, the names of Mary and John Pleasants appear on the list of the Chatham, Ontario. Vigilance Committee—a slave rescue organization led by Mary Ann Shadd Carey, William Day, and others. So, documents confirm these aspects of Pleasant's story.

Deed: Kent Land Registry fax 1993

Direct to I. D. Shadd, *Provincial Freeman* Office, Chatham, C.W.

Officers and Members of the Vigilance Committee: Wm. H. Day, Chairman; I. D. Shadd, Vice-Chairman; J. M. Bell,[8] Secretary; M. A. S. Cary, Assistant Secretary; H. C. Jackson,[9] Treasurer; L. S. Day,[10] T. F. Cary,[11] M. R. Delany,[12] J. H. Harris,[13] G. W. Brodie, J. Pleasant, M. E. Pleasant,[14] Mrs. I. D. Shadd,[15] O. Anderson. Collecting Agents: I. D. Shadd, Wm. H. Day, Mary A. S. Cary, J. H. Harris, G. W. Brodie, Lucy S. Day.

Gerrit Smith Banner (New York, N.Y.), 28 October 1858.

Ripley Document 73. Chatham Vigilance listing

In addition, one of Brown's sons and his daughter told Sam Davis in 1903 that they recalled a "colored woman" who gave funds to Brown in Canada. Wrote Davis,

> *John Brown still had some children living in California.... I hunted up Jason Brown.... When I stated my mission, he received me very cordially, "Yes," he said in response to my questions, "It is true my father went to Chatham in '58 and met a colored woman who advanced him considerable money. I don't know her name. I found Susan Brown, a daughter of John Brown living near Los Gatos.... She said that her father had met a colored woman in Chatham, Canada, and received considerable money from her to further the cause of emancipation, but he never disclosed her name...* (Davis 1903).

The children of Pleasant's closest associates, John A. Francis, Jr. and William Wilmore, Jr., also recalled that she collected funds from San Francisco citizens to give to Brown (JAFrans, 1935). Said Willmore, "She turned the money she had collected from Negroes into a draft before she set forth for Canada." (HH24: Willmore, Jr., 1938).

Thus, most of Pleasant's story is well supported, and, although my research shows that Pleasant did not give $30 or $40,000 of her own money to Brown as she claimed, it also shows that she intended to do so. As she claimed, Pleasant sent this amount to Nantucket for safekeeping with William C. Gardner, the eldest son of her former guardian; however, in 1858, when she wrote to request that money, Gardner wrote back, admitting that he had "lost" her funds (Gardner Dec.7, 1858). Said Gardner,

When I received your money from Mr. Kelly [Pleasant's San Francisco agent] I was worth at least $30,000 and no more thought of there being danger at not having it whenever you might want it than I thought of some other improbable thing.

The Mecklenburg Ride

Finally, Pleasant's claim that she returned home in 1858 and then returned in the Fall of 1859 to ride in advance of Brown onto Mecklenburg County plantations in southern Virginia has some support. Since there was no air travel then, Pleasant's claim to have gone home in December 1858 to manage her business finances and to have undertaken the same arduous trip East the following Fall has seemed implausible. African-American Museum and Library Curator Rick Moss, PhD., in the Bibbs' PBS documentary, *Meet Mary Pleasant (Mother of Civil Rights)* asked, "Why would she have done that?" "In the cause of liberty" was Pleasant's only reply (www.mepleasant.com).

She told Sam Davis and wrote in letters that, aided by a white abolitionist cohort who pretended to be her owner, she rode onto plantations disguised as a jockey (as she had in her early slave-alert days) to encourage slaves to support Brown's plan. Pleasant named the owners of the plantations on which she stopped (Comfort Magazine 1903) and chose this area because it contained the plantations with the largest number of slaves. Of course, John acted sooner than expected, and even though at least 300 slaves and freed men in the Harpers Ferry area still participated in the plan, the plan failed. Pleasant expressed frustration that her efforts her were in vain (MEP letter dictated to Mrs. S; Geffert 2002:602)

No one can produce an eye witness of this event, but the plantations named by Pleasant did exist, and the grandson of a slave on the Mark Alexander plantation—one named by Pleasant— calls her account extremely plausible because it was common for "Negro jockeys" to race on plantations in that area of the country, which was a racing center in Virginia (Bibbs/Smith emails 2004) and because Pleasant, having lived with her first husband in another racing center, Charles Town, W. Virginia, might have known the racing plantations in the state.

So, Pleasant may have made the perilous journey back to the East in 1859, without JJ, to participate personally. She was again the infamous jockey, this time determined to encourage the cautious slaves to support John's risky plan because she feared that, without preparation and alert, they would never chance insurrection and that the plan would fail. The person Mary trusted most was Mary, so it appears that this successful entrepreneur did indeed re-enter the grassroots of abolition to help John Brown (Davis/MEP letter, March 1902). Of course, Brown acted too soon; his plan was thwarted; his men (black and white) killed or scattered; he was hung, and Mary, whose note promising more funds was found on Brown's person, was forced to flee for her life! Mary later explained that this note with her initials on it—M.E.P. —promised more money for arms and caused her to be hunted. She claims to have hid out in New York to watch the papers on the matter but soon found that the signature was mistaken for W.E.P. So, her "bad writing" had saved her.

Pleasant's confirmed signature from a 1903 death-bed deposition

Her scribe Charlotte Dennis Downs confirmed in 1930 interviews with Helen Holdredge that Pleasant returned to San Francisco at the end of December of 1859. This scare, however, did not stop her efforts after her return to California. During the Civil War, she led the Franchise League against California secessionists. Said Mary of this episode in letter to her final biographer,

> *John said too much and John wrote too much, and there is nothin' that men live to regret more as what they write and set their names to... but I never regretted what I did for John Brown or for the cause of liberty for my race* (Davis Estate, Mar. 1902)

Chapter 13: The Later Years

Enduring Legacy

By 1863, the Emancipation Proclamation had allowed Mary Pleasant openly to declare her race, and she proudly recorded it as "Mary Pleasant, colored" in the City Directory. Then, she stepped forward to wage her boldest "civil-rights" battles. Records and legend indicate that her mentor, LaVeaux, had waged court battles for herself and others and that Pleasant had followed that use of the law in San Francisco. So, true to form, in 1863 after the law finally had granted people of color the right testify in court, she led her community in orchestrating court cases to test the new law. Martin Luther King would do something similar 100 years later, but understanding what came before is significant. Starting in 1863, Mary, leading the Franchise League, sought to test this new right in concert with groups all across the land.

According to civil-rights attorney David Oppenheimer, Mary most likely orchestrated three test cases against streetcar companies that routinely ejected blacks from their cars (Oppenheimer 1996). One case belonged to Charlotte Brown (the teenaged daughter of Pleasant's close friend, James E. Brown, Sr.) somewhat mistakenly today called "the 19th-century Rosa Parks." Two of these cases, however, belonged to Pleasant as plaintiff. All were either settled or won favorably by 1868.

However, the second of these (Pleasants vs. North Beach and Mission Railroad) went to the State Supreme Court where it lost its monetary award for pain and suffering (punitive damages), but set precedent. Because it went to the Supreme Court, this case could be cited by David

Oppenheimer in a 1982 civil-rights case (Commodore Homes) in that same high court. Pleasant's case, thus, helped to win the punitive damages for its plaintiff that Pleasant had been denied on appeal, and because it was the first time these damages had been won, Pleasant's case had helped change California Law! Today victims of discrimination can sue for and win punitive damages for discrimination. This case, was Pleasant's most enduring legacy (Bibbs/Oppenheimer 2003).

Free Enterprise

By the 1880's, both JJ and their only daughter (Elizabeth Smith Geary Peck) had passed away, and Pleasant with her partner, Thomas Bell—an officer of the Bank of California, went on to amass a $30,000,000 joint fortune, which Pleasant enjoyed and shared generously with those who were less fortunate (Pacific Appeal 1870, 71). Many have doubted the amount of this shared fortune, but Bell's records in the Bancroft Library and Pleasant's insolvency records and accounts in the Delaca papers suggest that it could be correct. The local papers, such as the Pacific Appeal and the San Francisco Examiner, have many stories of Pleasant's philanthropy in the 1870's, and in 1949 Sue Thurman recorded many recollections of Pleasant and her success in implementing her "Heritage of Power" for human rights. Said Thurman,

> *These things they [citizens] can remember perhaps—because the people who fight for freedom, for human rights, are always held in long and loving memory* (Thurman 1949).

They Scandalized Her Name

Of course, time and people change, and there came a time when New Orleaneans recalled little more than LaVeaux's composite legend and the fearsome power of her "hoodoo." There also came a time in San Francisco when citizens, white and black, recalled Pleasant only as a legendary caricature. They whispered about the cagey "madam," Mammy Pleasant, whom Pleasant's enemies and the Post Reconstruction tabloid press helped conjure (Teresa Bell diary 1899). Said Pleasant in a final deposition—

> *They paid the newspapers to malign and to vilify me and to blacken my character, but I did not reply to their assaults because I had staunch supports in the City and, so long as they supported me, I did not care one snap of one little finger for public opinion* (Deposition 1903).

But she did care more than pride would allow her to admit. We know because she tried three times to produce memoirs to offset these accusations only to have them ignored or suppressed by her enemies (Delaca/MEP-Davis letter 1903).

Pleasant's enemies were the powerful Senator William Sharon and her own partner's wife, Teresa Bell. Pleasant had opposed Sharon by backing the plaintiff, Missouri lass Sarah Althea Hill, in a scandalous court battle that was followed nationally in the daily press. Sharon, after having written letters declaring Sarah his common-law wife, sought to end their affair by ejecting Sarah from a suite in his Grand Hotel. To Pleasant, the contract was a Placage, and so she spent more than $63,000 on the case in behalf of this white, Southern damsel in distress. According to Pleasant, Sharon admitted to her privately that he had wronged Sarah, and he had tried to bribe Pleasant. When she refused, he insulted her, leading Pleasant to grow determined to defeat him (Davis/MEP1887; Deposition 1903). Sarah actually sued Senator Sharon (an unmarried widower) for divorce, thereby setting off a national scandal and a divorce trial, which the New York Times and other papers chronicled daily. Mary and Sarah first won, then lost, then won, and finally lost concurrent State and Federal versions of the case and its appeals. All of this lasted four years (1884-88) and brought devastation to all concerned.

Sharon died before the trials had concluded, but legend says that he asked his sons to seek revenge against Pleasant and that they did so in the press. Sarah lost her mind, and Mary lost her money and "good name"—the dearest price of all.

Mary's other enemy, Teresa Bell (Tress), was once her grateful, devoted protégé. Pleasant had rescued Tress from a seedy Dupont St (Grant St.) bordello. However, according to Teresa's diary, she grew lonely and envious of Pleasant as the years went by, especially over the deference that the adopted Bell children paid to Pleasant. Tress (Teresa Bell) is said to have tricked Tom Bell, Pleasant's secret lover, into marriage, but she never knew that Pleasant was using her marriage to Bell to cover her own relationship with him. After Bell's death in 1892, according to Tress's diaries and 1897 press accounts, she gradually became addicted to alcohol and opium, and estranged from society at large.

Soon after Bell's death Pleasant had declared bankruptcy to

circumvent creditors, and she secretly began removing her holdings from the Bell estate by having her first husband's niece, Rebecca Smith Boone, sign payment demands, which Tress, the legal owner, would pay. However, Tress accidentally uncovered this trickery, and after a week of angry exchanges, cast Mary Pleasant out of her own mansion. Of course, Pleasant had a ranch and a small apartment in San Francisco to meet her needs, but she was old, and Teresa's wealth blocked her efforts to reclaim her dignity.

Her old guard (her power base) had passed away, and she lost her home through a technicality in the courts when she tried to reclaim it. Before she died, Mary felt that San Francisco had closed a door on her and that no one seemed to recall her care and advocacy. She grew ill with heart failure. In truth, one of the adopted Bell children, Fred Bell, her good friend Sam Davis, and Olive Sherwood, a lawyer's wife who cared for the elderly, were there to help her. Some news articles praised and defended her (SF Examiner 10/13/1895; SF Call 1901) while others, such as the one engineered by Teresa and editor James E. Brown, Jr., destroyed her reputation (Bell Diary July 1899; SF Chronicle 7/9/1899). Those called her a blackmailer, baby stealer, murderess, madam, and swindler. "It was a time when the ship had to be righted," Dr. Rick Moss once said (MMP 2007). "Certainly," said author and scholar Shirley Ann Moore, "That 'mammy' appellation puts one in one's place. It consigns one to servitude."

Young Thomas Bell, Pleasant's partner, courtesy, SF History Ctr

Pleasant did not refute the charges directly, but in 1902 tried to counter them by publishing a memoir in a new paper, *The Pandex of the Press*, created for that purpose. Much of the one installment printed contains fabrications, such as birth in 1914 on 9 Barley St. in Philadelphia outside of slavery. However, a survey of records and Pleasant's other writings casts doubt on the date and disproves many of these assertions. For example, Barley St. did not exist in 1814! Clearly the account was designed to counter the accusations and demeaning attitudes that prevailed against her. However, Teresa bought the press and suppressed all other installments (Davis letter 1902).

So, the woman who was (in the 1870's) hailed as a great philanthropist, as an entrepreneur who had amassed a joint fortune and owned every type of business imaginable, as a champion of civil rights, was, by the early 1900's, reduced to the demeaning nickname, "Mammy Pleasant." Pleasant protested with characteristic, but heartfelt wit ("It gives me the suspiration!"), but, to her horror, the appellation and accusations stuck and are repeated to this day.

Caricature of Pleasant on the stand of the Sharon Trial

Mary Ellen Pleasant

Mother of Civil Rights
in California

Chapter 14: Epilogue

Remembrances

Mme. Marie LaVeaux died in 1881, poor, but surrounded by love. And, although confusion over the focus of her work with that of her successor, Marie II, still clouds her legacy, new books by Ina Fandrich, Carolyn Long, and others have emerged that clarify many of her true accomplishments. For the last 21 years of her life she too was in ill health. Still, she outlived both Eucharist (the daughter who briefly succeeded her) and Glapion, her beloved partner, by many years. In death, she too was both eulogized and mocked in the press. Now she is a New Orleans legend, and her New Orleans gravesite in St. Louis Cemetery #1 is marked with X's that designate it as a crossroads for the prayers of many petitioners.

After Pleasant's death, the reports of her enemies ultimately influenced 20th-century reportage and books. These confused modern-day scholars and cemented the demeaning nickname, "Mammy Pleasant." Pleasant also contributed to the confusion by writing false accounts of her birth and parentage and trying to "play it low" by pretending to be a servant in her own house to protect her personal life and assets. It was common knowledge that she had built that house, had been a wealthy woman, and was a friend of Thomas Bell, so her efforts only led to confusion and speculation and the label, "The house of mystery," being attached to her home. She was not madam or mammy, but she could not stop the legend. After her death on January 11 of 1904, she was eulogized for her generosity, but the scandals of the

1890's press echoed into the future to confound historians and obscure Pleasant's legacy.

Today, however the beauty and power of both Pleasant and her mentor, Mme. Marie LaVeaux, are being unfolded and celebrated, and there is renewed interest in their religious heritage, Vodou—now the national religion of Haiti (Teish 1985; Fanrich 1994; Warr III, 1964; Hudson 1996; Bibbs 1994-98, et al). Similarly TV specials now feature LaVeaux and her faith, and award-winning documentaries on Pleasant (by Bibbs) now show on PBS and have been seen in Canada and Europe (Bibbs 2007, 2008).

Moreover, although Mary Pleasant died feeling forgotten, she was ultimately remembered by "her City." In 1965, spearheaded by historians Sue B. Thurman, Ethel Nance, Helen Jones, Elena Albert, and others in The San Francisco Negro (now African-American) Historical and Cultural Society, the City of San Francisco, embedded a memorial medallion on the corner of Bush and Octavia Streets—the site of Pleasant's great mansion. In 1996 the trees there became City landmarks. The Negro Historical Society also placed a marker on Pleasant's grave, which is in a plot owned by the family of her final caretaker, Olive Sherwood. The cemetery marker, originally forged of wood, then marble from Pleasant's final residence, was replaced through the efforts of Tulocay Cemetery and the community at large in 2011 (Brennan, 2011; Hunnicutt, 2011). It holds a transcendent, award-winning sculpture by San Francisco artist Robert Alan Williams and is inscribed with the words, "Mary Ellen Pleasant, Mother of Civil Rights" and "She was a friend of John Brown," as Pleasant requested. Pleasant's memorial medallion in the City, however, is inscribed with the words—

Mary Ellen Pleasant, Mother of Civil Rights in California—a title that, according to historian Sue B. Thurman, Pleasant would most certainly earn again today—

> *If she were alive today, she would be in the forefront of the multitudes all over the world—men and women of every creed and nation—who labor with unerring insight in the high cause of human rights and human dignity* (Thurman 1949).

June 2011 dedication of the Pleasant grave marker, photo by the author

Modern Legacy

Mary Pleasant and her mentor, Marie LaVeaux, have left a modern legacy, and their work is continued today in the US and abroad by those who serve their communities locally, nationally, and internationally in positive ways across boundaries of race, class, and country. Among them, this book would like to honor a few initiates of African Traditional Religions who have inspired me: The "high" Mambo known as Mama Lola, who has served the US, Haiti, Benin, and New Orleans (where she is ably assisted by Brandi Kelley of Voodoo Authentica), Edo priestess-visual artist Nedra Williams (Ohen Imene), Yoruba initiates—Sankofa film actress-priest Oya Funmike Ogunlano, author-educator Halifu Osumare (Oyadamilola), and internationally renowned ritualistauthor-storyteller Luisah Teish (Iya Fa'jembola Fatunmise), who combines three traditions (Vodou, Ifá, and Lucumí) with Chieftaincies in Africa and Australia.

From the arts to academia, initiates continue to preserve the enduring and positive values of the religious heritage that enabled Marie LaVeaux to innovate and Mary Pleasant to become a Martin Luther King, a Malcolm X, and a Rosa Parks combined. Pleasant's ability to lead, to fight for liberty, to protect her people, and to love across boundaries of race and class without losing sight of her goals was outstanding. Those who do likewise reflect her heritage as well and stand on the shoulders of both Mary Pleasant and Marie LaVeaux. Egun Reo.

Pleasant Memorial medallion at Bush and Octavia Streets, San Francisco,
Photo by Adrian Ordañana

Appendices

Bibliography

Special notes:
This bibliography represents the references used in my quest to solve the mysteries of Mary Pleasant. It includes items in my private collection, which have been verified. Items with asterisks indicate proprietary works in private collections that I only have permission to excerpt in my work.

Notes on Special Collections
- The Delaca Estate* = The private collection held by Roxie Delaca, descendant of Olive Sherwood, Pleasant's final caretaker at the time of her death. Many items: letters, articles, records, depositions, willed to Sherwood in Pleasant's last effects
- The Helen Holdredge Collection (HH) = an item of The Helen Holdredge.
"Mammy Pleasant" Collection in the San Francisco History Center of the San Francisco Main Public Library—contains witnessed, transcribed interviews and interview notes on close associates of Pleasant. These are found in ledgers 24, 25, 26, and 26A, which have dated, rather than numbered pages. These interviews, when correlated, can create a credible reference for an event in Pleasant's life.
- The Helen Holdredge Estate* = ledgers with interviews by Liga Foley, the alleged granddaughter of
   Marie LaVeaux, and Charlotte Dennis Downs, Pleasant's scribe in a private home. Bibbs has the only
   excerpts.
- The Davis Estate =
   — The 1901/02 manuscripts dictated/written to Nevada writer/legislator Sam Davis for publication in The Pandex of the Press, a new San Francisco newspaper. Only one part of this three-part document was ever published, although accounts from it form the basis of a couple of Sam Davis' 1903, 04 published articles on Pleasant.
   — Letters in that collection between Pleasant and Sam Davis
   — Extant autobiographical accounts that Mary Ellen Pleasant dictated to 1) Emma Kaiser (ca. 1887) or 2) Sam Davis (1901, 1902). They differ in certain facts, so the job of this research has been to uncover the "truth" of these memoirs. All of these manuscripts contain misstatements and inconsistencies and have to be correlated/researched carefully against historical and vital records.
- The Bibbs Collection = The research collection of Susheel Bibbs, which was verified by the Director of the California Council for the Humanites in 1999. Under agreements with the original owners, copies made for Bibbs from other private

157

collections (memoirs, letters, interviews, etc.) may only be used in her work.

-Carolyn M. Long Collection., Private Collection on Marie LaVeaux. Documents/ Unpublished Articles collected by this author of works on Marie LaVeaux. Washington. DC.

Unpublished Sources

Records

Philadelphia Archdiocese Cemetery Records sent to the author: 2/1994

Cincinnati Census: 1810: 32; 1820:87

Property Deed for Lots # 8 and 9 on Campbell Ave. (Township of Harwich). Chatham, Ontario: Kent Land Registry, Ministry of Consumer and Commercial Relations. 1858, 1872. Sheets 45, 48, 49

"John J. Pleasants and Mary E.vs. North Beach and Mission R.R. Company." Transcript on Appeal. San Francisco: Alta California Printing House: 1867

San Francisco Census 1890 for The Bell Household. Ward 12: 126

San Francisco City Directories. 1859, 1863

Ships Passage Records: San Francisco, vol. 3: 137-140

"Ship's Passage Records." Ledger 26. Helen Holdredge Collection. San Francisco Public Library History Center: 4/27/21

"Ships Passage Records." Press Democrat and Times Picayunne Newspapers. New Orleans. Microfiche. 1790-1881

The Papers of Thomas Bell. Bancroft Library. Berkeley, CA: University of California at Berkeley

Vital Records Searched: City Directories, birth, death, baptismal, sailing and census records (1830-50) in the following collections: Boston Public and Archdiocese, Oakland Public Library News Archive, Benton, MO: Public Library, Benton Cemetery. Bureau of Land Records, Ontario, Canada. Honolulu: Queen Emma Collection, Benton Museum. Kansas Historical Society Archives. New Orleans: New Orleans Archdiocese and Maritime Archives 1819-1881, New Orleans Public Library, Historic New Orleans Collection, Historic New Orleans Voodoo Museum. New York: Maritime and Main Public Libraries. Nantucket, MA: Nantucket History Association Archives, Folger School/Museum, Maritime Museum. Philadelphia Public Library Census Records, Archdiocese Cemetery Records. Sacramento: California State Library. San Bruno: The National Archives. San Francisco: Bureau of Vital Records, Main Library History Center, Maritime Library, Sutro Library. St. Louis: Missouri History Society Archive, St. Louis Public Library.

Private Collections (Primary and Secondary)

Helen Holdredge Estate, Los Angeles. Charlotte Dennis Downs Interviews 1930: 6, 10. 11, and un-numbered pages

_____: Liga Foley Interviews. 1939: 24 and un-numbered pages

Delaca Estate, Vallejo, CA: Thomas Gardner. Letter to Olive Sherwood. Vallejo. CA. 1906.

_____: William C. Gardner Letters to Mary Ellen Pleasant. Vallejo, CA 1858: 11/23/1863,

_____: Mary Ellen Pleasant. Insolvency Papers.

_____: Mary Ellen Pleasant: Letter dictated to Mrs. S. [Sherwood]: undated six-page fragment

_____: Mary Ellen Pleasant. Memoir. ca.1880 dictated to Kaiser, Emma: 1, 8. Davis-Crowell Estate, Carson City, NV-Los Angeles: Mary Ellen Pleasant. Memoir Manuscripts: 1887, 1901-1902. dictated to Sam P. Davis. vol. 1, 2.

_____: Sam P. Davis. Letter to Mary Pleasant: 3/17/1902

_____: Mary Ellen Pleasant. "Second Marriage." Memoir Manuscript. 1902. ed. Sam P. Davis. vol 2: 1-5

_____: _____. Letter to Sam P. Davis: Mar. 17, 1902.

Bibbs Collection, Sacramento: Interviews and Notes by the author:

_____: Atanda, Chief Aare Olalekan. Ifa. Lecture notes by the author. San Francisco: Center for African and African-American Culture. November 4, 1998

_____: Bibbs, Susheel, Ph.D. Liga Foley. Research-presentation Manuscript. Louisiana State Museum: 10/27/1997

_____: Fandrich, Ina. Ph.D. Emails/phone-conference notes to the author: April 21, 1998, 10/1997-5/1998

_____: Fatunmbi, Awa Fa'Lokun, Interviews by the author on Ifa. 1994, 1998

_____: Smith, Lloyd. Emails on Mecklenburg County and Mary sent to the author: 4/9/2002.

_____: San Francisco Ships Passage Records. The San Francisco History Room. San Francisco Main Library. vol. 3:137,140

_____: Libby, Jean. "John Brown's Plan." San Francisco: Interview by the author 2003.

_____: Long, Carolyn M. Email to the author on Marie LaVeaux: 3-38-98. others: 10/97-5/98.

_____: Maes-Valdez, Xochipala (Iyanifa Fakayode). Interview by the author 1998

_____: McGlone, Robert E. Phd. University of Hawaii at Manoa. Interview by the author by phone 1955. p.2.

_____: Milan, Mary. Email/Phone interviews by the author on Vodou and Marie LaVeaux. 1998

_____: Oppenheimer, David. San Francisco: Letter dated 1996.

_____: Osumare. Halifu Ph.D. Katherine Dunham. Interview by the author 2006

_____ The Aesthetic of the Cool. Lecture notes by the author. U.C. Berkeley Diaspora Conference April 1998.

_____: Saraswati. Swami Dayananda. The Bhagavad Gita. . Lecture Notes by the author. Mumbai, India: Sandeepany Sadhanalaya 1978.

_____: Smith, Lloyd. Emails to the author: 2/5/2004, 2/6/2004.

_____: Teish. Luisah (Iyanifa Fa'jembola). Vodun and Diaspora Traditions. Interviews by the author. Marie LaVeaux and New Orleans Vodou. Interviews by the author. Oakland, CA 1993, 1997
_____: Thurman, Sue B. Interview by the author. San Francisco 1996
_____: "Interviews on Marie LaVeaux" Folio 25. The Federal Writer's Project. Baton Rouge: N. Louisiana State University 1930

Dissertations/Studies
Broussard, Albert S. Report: Civil Rights, Racial Protest, and Anti-slavery Activism in San Francisco 1850-1865. Commissioned by the National Park Service 2000
Conrich, Lloyd. The Mammy Pleasant Legend, San Francisco: The San Francisco African American Historical and Cultural Society Library
Fandrich, Ina. Ph.D. Dissertation: The Mysterious Voodoo Queen. Marie LaVeaux 1994. Temple University. UMI Microfilms: 2, 15, 18, 78, 79, 200, 210, 211, 242, 251, 260, 266, 304
Hudson, Lynn M. When Mammy Became A Millionaire. Mary Ellen Pleasant, An African American Entrepreneur. Ph.D. dissertation. Indian University 1996
Long, Carolyn M. Collection: Article: Untitled. Marie Laveau. 1997: 54. Washington. D.C.
McBratney, M.. Masters Thesis: Honoring and Initiation of the Priestess in Post Modern-day Society. Oakland: University of Creation Spirituality. 1998. Chapter 2: 24
Warr, Jesse, III. In Search of "Mammy Pleasant." June 1975. Research Paper for History 285-D. University of California at Berkeley: 4

Publicly Held/Published Sources
Holdredge Collection. San Francisco Main Library History Center:
            Ledger 24 Interviews with Harold Camba: 22. Charlotte Downs: 34-36. John Allen Francis, Jr: 50, 141. Lane: 90, 93. Atty. John L. McNab: 112. Lucy Ritzman: 139. David Ruggles, Jr: 5. 6. 141. 145. William Willmore, Jr: 24.
_____. Ledger 25. Interview with Vina Dyer. Helen Holdredge Collection: 3/18/15
_____. Ledger 26. Interviews with Atty. Eduard Bergner: 4/8/21, 4/12/21, 9/17/21, 9/28/21, those dated 1934:3 and 1954. Charlotte Downs: 9/6/21, 11/10/21. William Willmore, Jr: 4/20/21, 6/13/21-6/24/21, 10/3/21, Typed pages 3-15, 17, 19 and 1938: 9/28/21

Newspapers/Journal Interviews
"Autobiography of Mary Pleasant." Pandex of the Press, vol 1. San Francisco. ed. Sam P. Davis 1902
Davis-Crowell Estate: Davis, Sam P. "How a Colored Woman Aided John Brown."

Comfort Magazine. November 1903: 3

_____. "Autobiography of Mary Ellen Pleasant. Part 1." Pandex of the Press 1902:1

Dorsey, Lilith. "Interview with Carlos Montenegro." Oshun. vol. 3. Issue 2. Summer 1998: 5-7

Fraser, Isobel. "Mammy Pleasant, The Woman." The SF Call. 12/29/01: 2

Hunnicut, Trevor, "Marker for 'Mother of Civil Rights in California." San Francisco Chronicle (Datebook). 6/27/2011: 1

"Interview with Mary Pleasant." The SF Examiner: 10/13/1895

"Obituary of Marie LaVeaux." New Orleans: Louisiana Press Democrat: 6/17/1881

"Obituary of Marie LaVeaux." New Orleans: Weekly Picayune: 6/17/1881

"Obituary of Marie LaVeaux." New Orleans: The Daily States: 6/17/1881

Articles and Monographs

Doyle, Jim. "Gold Rush Paved Way to Freedom." San Francisco Chronicle/Contra Costa. July 18, 1998: A15

Geggus, David. "Haitian Voodoo in the Eighteenth Century: Language. Culture. Resistence." Jarbuch fur Geschichte von Staadt. Wirkschaft und Gesellschaft Lateinamerikas 28. 1991: 8-13, 27. also data tables 12, 15

Geffert, Hannah, "John Brown and His Black Allies – An Ignored Alliance." The Pennsylvania Magazine of History and Biography. Vol. CXXVI. No. 4. October 2002: 592- 610.

Hamilton, James C. Monograph: "John Brown in Canada." Canadian Magazine. December 1894: 11.

LeBlanc, Joyce. "Strange Rumblings in the Night." Journal Unknown. New Orleans: Amistad Collection. Tulane University

Nevadomsky, Joseph. "The Initiation of A Priestess -- Olokun Initiation." Journal Unknown. courtesy Luisah Teish: 188-191, 202, 206

Touchstone, Blake. "Voodoo in New Orleans." Louisiana History. vol. 13, no. 4. Fall 1972: 371-385

Compilations/Books

Abimbola, Wande. Ph.D. Ifa. An Exposition of Ifa Literary Corpus. Boston: Athelia Henrietta Press. 1997 (a): 13, 14,18-25, 32, 33

_____. Ifa Will Mend Our Broken World. Boston: Athelia Henrietta Press. 1997(b): 22, 33, 72, 83-89, 106-107.

Alrocchi, Julia. The Spectacular San Franciscans; Dutton 1940

Adams, Boniface. The Gift of Religious Leadership. New Orleans: Archdiocese Archives: 360-367

Asbury, Herbert. The French Quarter. NY: Garden City Publishing. 1938: 229-262

Awolalu, J. Omosade. Yoruba Beliefs and Sacrificial Rites. Athelia Henrietta Press 1996: 1, 5

Bascom, William, Ph.D. Ifa Divination. Bloomington: Indiana University Press 1991: 3-11, 26

Blier. Patricia. Ph.D. African Vodun. Chicago: University of Chicago Press 1995: 38-40

Beasley, Delilah. Negro Trailblazers 1919: 95

Bennett, Lerone. "Frederick Douglass: Learn Trades of Starve 1853." Before the Mayflower. Johnson Publications. 6th ed.

Blassingame, John W. Black New Orleans. University of Chicago Press 1973: 13-18

Bracey, Susan L. Life by the Roaring Roanoke. The Mecklenburg County Bicentennial Commission 1977: 158, 271

Bodin, Ron. Voodoo Past and Present. Lafayette: Center for Louisiana Studies. University of SW Louisiana.

Brandon. George. Ph.D. Santeria. from Africa to the New World. Bloomington: Indiana University Press. 1993: 13, 15, 18, 23, 176-184

Broussard, Albert, Black San Francisco, 1993

Brown, Karen McCarthy, Ph.D. Mama Lola. Berkeley: University of California Press 1990. 2001: 13, 31, 113, 215-217, 273-280, 320-326, 351, 352

Chinmayananda. H.H. Swami. Chapter 3. The Bhagavad Gita. Bombay: Chinmaya Publications 1984.

Conrad, Earl. "She Was A Friend of John Brown." Negro World Digest Circa 1949: 7-11.

Courlander, Harold. Haiti Singing. Chapel Hill. NC: University of N. Carolina Press. 1939: 27, 36, 50, 98-100

Daniel, Yvonne. Dancing Wisdom. University of Illinois Press 2004: 56

Davis, Sam P. "How a Colored Woman Aided John Brown." Maine: Comfort Magazine 1903: 3

Deren, Maya. Divine Horsemen. Kingston. NY: McPherson and Co.. 2nd ed. 1953: 16, 17

Desmangles, Leslie, Ph.D. Faces of the Gods. Philadelphia: Temple University Press 1992: 2-11, 24-29, 34-37, 63-64, 75

Dessosiers, Toulouse. Unnamed 1970 35-39

Drewal, Margaret, Ph.D. Yoruba Ritual. Bloomington: Indiana University Press 1984. xv, xix, 4

De T Abajian, James, San Francisco Walking Tour. San Francisco African American Historical and Cultural Society 1974

_____. Blacks in the Selected Western Newspapers. San Francisco African American Historical and Cultural Society.

Eames, David, SF Street Secrets; Gem Guides, 1995.

Epega, Afolabe A. and Newmark, Phillip John. The Sacred Ifa Oracle. HarperSan Francisco 1994

Fandrich, Ina J. Ph.D.. The Mysterious Voodoo Queen. Marie Laveaux. New York/London: Routledge 2005: 68, 255, note 4

Fatunmbi, Awo Fa'lokun. Awo Bronx: Original Publications 1992: 1, 8, 22, 23, 94 108-111

Fatunmbi, Awo Fa'lokun. Iwa Pele. Bronx: Original Publications 1991: 84, 85, 102-112, 120

Fatunmbi, Awo Fa'lokun. Iba'se Orisa. Bronx: Original Publications 1994

Fatunmbi, Awo Fa'lokun. Ori. Bronx: Original Publications 2005

Galembo, Phyllis. Vodou. Berkeley: Ten Speed Press 1998: iv-xviii, xxi-xxii

Gould, Milton S. A Cast of Hawks. La Jolla: Copley Books. 1985. p. 187.

Hansen, Gladys, SF Almanac; Chronicle Books 1975

Haskins, Jim. Voodoo and Hoodoo. Bronx: Original Publications 2nd ed. 1992: 59

Herskovits, Melville and Francis S.. Dahomean Narrative. Evanston: Northwestern University Press 1953: 179-190

Hudson, Lynn. "John Brown." The Making of Mammy Pleasant. University of Illinois Press 2003

Hussey, Christopher and Mary. Nantucket History 1903

Hittell History of San Francisco 1878

Hurbon, Laennec. Voodoo. Search for the Spirit. New York: Abrams. Inc. Publishers 1995: 13-16, 21, 26, 31, 70-83, 108-115, 142, 144

Jones, Ava Kay. Principles of the use of Gris Gris Bags. Potions. and Dolls. New Orleans: Voodoo Macuumba. Undated

Kaiso. Clark, Veve, Ph.D. and Johnson, Sara E., editors. University of Wisconsin Press 2005: 112, 424, 425, 625, 629.

Katz, William Lorenz. The Black West. Seattle: Open Hand Publishing, Inc. 1973: 41-170

Kroninger, Robert. Sarah and the Senator. North Press 1964

Lancaster, Clay. Nantucket in the Nineteenth Century; Dover, 1979

Lapp, Rudolph M. Afro-Americans in California. 2" Ed., San Francisco: Boyd & Fraser Publishing Co., 1987: 11-13.

_____Blacks in Gold Rush California. New Haven: Yale Press. 1977: 126-157

Lewis, Oscar. Bonanza Inn, New York: Knopf 1939

_____. Sea Routes to the Gold Fields, New York: Knopf 1949

Libby, Jean et al. John Brown Mysteries. Allies for Freedom. 1999: 14, 18, 20

Lockwood, Charles. Suddenly San Francisco. SF: Examiner Books, 1978

Long, Carolyn M. A New Orleans Voudou Priestess, The Legend and Reality of Marie Laveaux. Tallahassee: University Press of Florida. 2006.

Long, Carolyn M. Spiritual Merchants. University of Tennessee Press. Knoxville. 2001. p. 37.

MacDonald, Robert R. et al (compilation): Carter, Doris D, "The African Presence in Colonial Louisiana": 163-189. Fiehrer, Thomas M. "Refusing to Relinquish the Struggle": 3-31. Taylor, Joe Gray "A New Look at Slavery in Louisiana":191-208. Rankin, David C. "The Politics of Caste": 118-129. Vincent, Charles. "Black Louisianans During the Civil War and Reconstruction": 98-106 Louisiana's Black Heritage. New Orleans: Louisiana State Museum. 1979: 163-189

McEvedy, Colin. The Penguin Atlas of African History. New York: Penguin Books 1995: 38, 76, 95

McGowan, R. 108, 176-177

Metraux, Alfred. Voodoo in Haiti. 1972: 64-69, 88-91, 151-191. 305-322

Rankin, J. 1979:118

Schneider, Jimmie, Quicksilver; New Almaden, CA: Schneider 1992.

Somé, Malidoma. Of Water and Spirit. New York: Penguin Books 1994:11, 52,53

Tallant. Robert. Voodoo in New Orleans. 1946.

Teish. Luisah (Iya Fajembola Fatunmise). Jambalaya. Harper San Francisco 1985:111

_____. Carnival of the Spirit. HarperSF 1997: 143

Templeton, John, Our Roots Run Deep; Electron Access 1993

Thompson, Robert Farris. Flash of the Spirit. New York: Vintage Books. 1984: 9-11, 16, 17

Thurman, Sue B. "Mary Ellen Pleasant." Pioneers of Negro Origin in California. Acme Press 1949

Wheeler, B. Gordon, Ph. D. Black California. New York: Hippocrene Books. 1993: 87-109, 122

Media Sources

Brennan, Nancy. "Civil Rights Figure Honored at Tulocay." NapaValleyRegister. com. June 11, 2011. http://napavalleyregister.com/news/local/civil-rights-figure-honored-at-tulocay-cemetery/article_e1fdfa70-949d-11e0-b77c-001cc4c03286. html

Bibbs, Susheel. Meet Mary Pleasant—Mother of Civil Rights. Documentary Film. First Broadcast on PBS 1/2008. Sacramento: M.E.P. Productions: www. mepleasant.com.

_____. "The Legacies of Mary Ellen Pleasant." Viewfinder. Sacramento: KVIE-TV, March 2007

_____. Meet Mary Pleasant DVD Archive. vols. 1 and 2. Video Interviews by the author with Kartunnen, Francis. PhD.; Robinson, Gwendolyn (Chatham, Ontario); Moss, Rick, PhD.; Moore, Shirley Ann, PhD. Oakland: The African-America Museum and Library. 2003, 2007.

_____. "Voodoo" Bibbs'Video Archive. Interviews by the author with Teish, Luisah 1993, 1996. Jones, Ava Kay. Gandolfo, Gerald 1996. Fatumnbi, Awo Fa'Lokun 1994, 1998. Glover, Elmer. Priestess Miriam. Coco 1996; Kelley, Brandi 1995, 1996. Millan, Mary 1997

_____. De Caro, Louis. Ph.D. "John Brown's Plan." John Brown DVD. New York: Interview by the author: 2003. M.E.P. Productions. www.mepleasant.com.

_____. Libby, Jean on "John Brown's Plan." John Brown DVD. New York: Interview by the author: 2003. M.E.P. Productions. www.mepleasant.com.

_____. "Oppenheimer, David on Mary Pleasant cases." San Francisco: Interview by the author, 2003. "The Legacy of Mary Ellen Pleasant." Viewfinder Series. KVIE-TV, PBS, Sacramento by M.E.P. Productions 3/2007, and Meet Mary Pleasant—Mother of Civil Rights. Documentary Film. First Broadcast, PBS 1/2008. Sacramento: M.E.P. Productions:www.mepleasant.com.

Gates, Henry Louis Ph.D. Black in Latin America: Haiti. CNN. May 2011

Hall, Gwendolyn. Ph.D. Database: "In Search of the Invisible Africans." Louisiana Slave Database (1723-1820) 1998:8

Hunnicut, Trevor, "Marker for 'mother of civil rights in California.'" SFGate.com. San Francisco Chronicle Datebook, June 27, 2011. http://www.sfgate.com/cgi-bin/article.cgi?f=/c/a/2011/06/27/DDPI1K1ELS.DTL

Lovinsky, Alourdes (Mama Lola). "Voodoo" Meet Mary Pleasant DVD Archive. Interview by the author. 2003

Documentary: In Search of History -- Voodoo Secrets. The History Channel. 1998. #AAE-74036

Documentary: "Divine Drumbeats-- Katherine Dunham and Her People." Dance in America. Public Broadcasting, 1965

Brief Biography: Susheel Bibbs

Bibbs as Pleasant (photo by Jim Dennis, San Francisco) in Meet Mary Pleasant, the PBS film and one-woman. Chautauquas. Bibbs in a photo by Marshall Bailey of Sacramento.

Filmmaker, scholar, performer Susheel Bibbs, who lectured for many years at U.C. Berkeley, holds a masters degree in Vocal Performance, and a PhD in Communications, emphasizing the Mass Communication of African-American and Diaspora History. Since 1991 Bibbs has researched Mary Pleasant, and in 1999 she was named "the world's foremost expert on Pleasant" in a "Highest Commendation," given by San Francisco Supervisors. Bibbs has authored books, a DVD archive, articles, and film documentaries on Pleasant and has created acclaimed one-woman enactments (chautauquas), which have toured internationally. They have been included on the touring rosters of the California Humanities and the Network-to-Freedom Program of the National Parks Service. In media, Bibbs received broadcast awards and a national Emmy when she was a Public Television Executive Producer for WGBH-Boston. As an independent film producer, she has won festival and broadcast awards for her documentaries on Mary Ellen Pleasant—among them a California Silver Telly, Best Director of a Documentary, and the Gold Kahuna Award for Excellence in Filmmaking from the Honolulu International Film Festival. A recipient of many grants, she is has been sponsored fiscally by The Bay Area Video Coalition, The Film Arts Foundation, and The San Francisco Film Society. Her film

Heritage of Power

Meet Mary Pleasant, Mother of Civil Rights in California has been shown on PBS, in Canada, and at The Cannes Film Festival. Bibbs' works and schedule can be found through the M.E.P. Productions-Daya Kay Communications Web site —www.mepleasant.com.

Index

A

Abimbola, Wande 65, 67, 78
abolition 3, 12, 14, 18, 114, 142
abolitionist 12, 13, 14, 98, 115, 135
Africa 44, 45, 47, 48, 51, 56, 58, 60, 64, 67, 74, 86, 94, 121, 152
African i, 1, 2, 3, 5, 6, 33, 34, 37, 41, 42, 43, 45, 46, 48, 50, 52, 53, 55, 56, 57, 58, 59, 60, 61, 62, 63, 64, 65, 66, 67, 68, 69, 70, 75, 78, 81, 82, 84, 86, 87, 88, 90, 103, 106, 107, 121, 141, 152, 156, 169
Africans 49, 56, 61, 64, 66, 86
Agwe Twoyo 48
Aido Wedo 45
ancestor spirits 45, 50, 59
Angola 56, 67
Atibon 47
Ayedo Wedo 45
Ayida Wedo 45, 46, 50, 57, 75
Azaka 48
Azili river 48

B

Bade 48
Bakongo 50, 52, 58
BaKongo Nzambi 75
Bambara 50, 52
Bantu 52, 56
Baron Samedi 48
Bell, Fred 149
Bell, Teresa 147, 148
Bell, Thomas 123, 146, 155
Benin 44, 45, 48, 66, 74, 75, 93
Bhagavad Gita 85
Black Codes 35, 37, 53
Bondye 45, 46, 49, 53
Bondyé 93
bordellos 127, 128
Boston 6, 12, 14, 65
Bragg, Tom 31
Brazil 47, 101
Brown, Charlotte 145
Brown, John 135, 136, 138, 140, 142, 143
Buntu 56

Made in the USA
Charleston, SC
21 January 2016